MW01102290

SOCIAL ISSUES

Meditative Thinking
and the Threefold Social Order

SOCIAL ISSUES

Meditative Thinking
and the Threefold Social Order

Rudolf Steiner

Translated by Joe Reuter

Translation revised by Sabine H. Seiler

Anthroposophic Press

This book is a translation of the first five lectures of
Vom Einheitsstaat zum dreigliedrigen sozialen Organismus,
volume 334 in the Collected Works,
published by Rudolf Steiner Verlag, Dornach, Switzerland, 1983.

Published in the United States by Anthroposophic Press,
R.R. 4, Box 94 A1, Hudson, New York 12534.

Library of Congress Cataloging-in-Publishing Data

Steiner, Rudolf, 1861–1925.
  [Vom Einheitsstaat zum dreigliedrigen sozialen Organismus.
Vorlesungen 1–5. English]
  Social issues : meditative thinking and the threefold social order /
Rudolf Steiner ; translated by Joe Reuter ;
translation revised by Sabine H. Seiler.
      p. cm.
  Translation of: Vom Einheitsstaat zum dreigliedrigen sozialen
Organismus. Vorlesungen 1–5.
  Includes bibliographical references.
  ISBN 0-88010-359-0 : $24.95. — ISBN 0-88010-358-2 (pbk) : $12.95
  1. Anthroposophy. 2. Social problems. I. Title.
BP595.S894V65   1991   91-29399
299' .935Òdc20   CIP

10 9 8 7 6 5 4 3 2 1

Printed in the United States of America

Contents

Foreword

In 1920, two years after the armistice that ended World War I, Europe was still in turmoil. The old political and social order had tumbled, and a new order had not yet been found. The Central European nations, buffeted by various political and social movements claiming to represent the path to a better future, seemed to drift toward an economic catastrophe. Exhausted by the struggle to make a living in a ravaged economy, people hardly knew where to turn for political leadership and the rebuilding of society. This is the situation—not all that different from our own seventy years later—in which Rudolf Steiner presented his vision of a new, threefold social order.

What Steiner offers is not another social program or government-sponsored band-aid solution to social and economic ills. Rather, the threefold social order entails a complete restructuring and reorganization of the various spheres making up modern society. What is more— and this makes this social order particularly relevant and interesting for our time— the threefold social order builds on the foundation of a new understanding of the individual as a spirit-being.

As Steiner carefully and convincingly explains in these lectures, once the spiritual view of the human being has been accepted, all our social institutions and structures will necessarily have to change because they have grown out of the way we define what it means to be human and to live in a community with other human beings. Consequently, education, politics, and even the legal system will have to be transformed in accordance with this new understanding.

This is an exciting and difficult undertaking. As Steiner explains, the change will have to take place both within the individual and in the outer structure of society as well. In the lectures gathered in this volume, Steiner points the way to this necessary transformation. His passionate and forceful tone, born out of a deep understanding of the suffering caused by the old, materialistic order, conveys the urgency of the problems and the dire need for a change.

Of the many lectures by Steiner I have read, edited, or translated, these are certainly among the most revolutionary and exciting. While the situation Steiner describes here may seem merely historical, it is strangely similar to our own. In fact, these lectures have a timeless relevancy: as long as materialism is not overcome through a spiritual understanding of the human being, similar problems will recur in one form or another. Set against the grim background of the post-World War I years, these lectures are for us a beacon of hope for a better, spirit-filled future.

Sabine H.Seiler

Introduction

These lectures can be a valuable aid for anyone sufficiently distressed by outer social conditions to want to do
something about them. Certainly, if taken up in the way
they were intended, they can stimulate a reader to cultivate
"spiritual activism," that is, the development of inner spiritual capacities which may then be used to bring about the
renewal of outer social life. Many people today are dissatisfied and suffer from emptiness of soul because of the
materialistic, profit-oriented society in which they live. To
find comfort and relief, they seek a spiritual path to soothe
their battered souls. Those who seek a spiritual path
merely for comfort of soul may find these lectures unset-
tling. They are not meant for comfort and solace. They are
meant for resolve and action. To take up their content
means work: rigorous, systematic, inner work.

In these lectures, Rudolf Steiner describes how human
beings can change their inner, spiritual lives in a way that
can lead to the transformation of destructive elements in
our social institutions. The idea that what we confront in
our external lives originates in the inner life of individual
men and women is not unique to Steiner. What is unique
in these lectures is "anthroposophy." This is the name that
Steiner gives both to the method of self-transformation
that he proposes and to the view of the human being and
the cosmos attainable by this method.

Anthroposophy describes the human being as consisting of body, soul, and spirit and holds the cosmos and all matter to be a manfestation of spiritual worlds. It is the modern form of a spiritual science which Steiner traces back to the prehistoric mystery centers of the East. He points out that in these ancient mystery centers, "science, art, and religion were not distinct, but unified" and "the goal of education was not simply to help students develop their thinking, feeling, and sensitivity, so that knowledge of their connection to a spiritual world would satisfy them. No, in addition to enabling them to form a worldview [in which science, art, and religion were united], their education was intended to develop their capacities for directing the outer, practical, and social concerns of their community."

What the ancient mystery centers accomplished then, anthroposophical spiritual science seeks to accomplish now, a worldview that unites art, science, and religion—one from which it is possible to develop the requisite inner capacities that can lead to change in our social life.

In the ancient East, human beings recognized, and felt instinctively connected to, spiritual worlds. As human consciousness evolved, this instinctive connection and recognition has been lost. Modern natural science, which focuses exclusively on the physical world, denies the possibility of any objective access to the spiritual worlds, even if these are a reality. Spiritual science, on the other hand, utilizes the scientific method to investigate the spiritual worlds that underlie all matter. In Steiner's view, the methods and results of research in anthroposophical spiritual science are as systematic and reliable as those of modern materialistic science.

From this point of view, experimentation and the systematic observation of nature are to modern natural science what the systematic working through of inner exercises and meditations are to anthroposophy. These inner exercises begin with the observation and control of thought life. Instead of divesting thinking of all feeling and will in order to gain objectivity (as is the case in modern science), Steiner says that we must imbue our thinking with refined feeling and directed will in such a way that it remains objective. Properly schooled, thinking, by means of meditative exercises, can develop into a faculty of spiritual perception.

Knowledge of Higher Worlds and Its Attainment, referred to in these lectures, gives inner exercises for the gradual transformation of the subjective, instinctual will into a will directed by the higher self. Exercises are also given in that book for the purification of instinctual feelings and their transformation or elevation to objective organs of perception. By these means the negative, subjective characteristics often associated with feelings and will are overcome. This is particularly important in the social sphere. For it is above all in social issues and human relations that abstract thinking devoid of all feeling and will is destructive, because everyone rests on his or her own particular viewpoint. When feelings and will are left out, everyone is perfectly correct in his or her standpoint, yet no living connection between people is possible.

Reading these lectures makes it painfully clear that one cannot rightfully call oneself a student of anthroposophy without doing these exercises, anymore than one could call onself a student of biology or physics without applying oneself to the rigors of systematic experimentation and observation. Here, indeed, is one reason why the results of spiritual science have had so little impact on our lives. To understand why this is so, think of what would happen if students of biology or physics decided to give up all experimentation and research and merely read and contemplated past discoveries. Of course, as Steiner states, not everyone needs to consciously transform his or her inner life through spiritual exercises. Nevertheless, if spiritual science is to have any impact on outer life, there has to be a sufficient number of people who do.

For the sensitive reader of these lectures, therefore, nagging questions arise, such as, Who will take up this work in an active way? and, more specifically, Should I overcome all the obstacles in my life and become active inwardly?

Elsewhere, Steiner states that one of the ways to verify the results of spiritual scientific research is to examine whether they agree with one another and with the facts and experiences of outer life. In these lectures, he gives a panoramic overview of the mission of anthroposophy, one that reveals the connections between his basic works on philosophy, social renewal, and inner development and the spiritual nature of the human being. These basic works present different aspects of the same, fundamental spiritual reality. Dive into the depths of any one of them and myriad connections will be found to the others. Penetrate, for example, *The Philosophy of Freedom* (or *Spiritual Activity*), and you come to the exercises of thought control in *Knowledge of the Higher Worlds* or the necessity of cultural freedom in *Towards Social Renewal*. Or penetrate the essence of democracy in *Towards Social Renewal* and you find a connection to the exercises for the refinement of feelings in *Knowledge of the Higher Worlds*. Thus, one of the functions of these lectures is to direct the reader toward the study and practice outlined in these basic books.

From a certain point of view, it is perhaps unfortunate that so many of Rudolf Steiner's lecture cycles were written down and later published (something he, initially, did not intend). For the consequence of this has been that fundamental written texts such as *The Philosophy of Freedom (Spiritual Activity)*, *Theosophy*, *Knowledge of the Higher Worlds and Its Attainment*, *An Outline of Occult Science*, and *Towards Social Renewal* are lost in a sea of literally hundreds of printed lecture cycles. The only way properly to absorb the results of the spiritual scientific research contained in these lecture cycles is continually and repeatedly to work through these basic books. The necessity and reason for doing this is expanded and reinforced throughout these lectures.

Against this background and with this intention readers will gain from the lectures printed here an understanding of the uniqueness of anthroposophical spiritual science as a means of understanding oneself and the cosmos. That is to say, we will begin to understand how science and religion, now separated, can be brought together again through spiritual scientific investigation.

Many people today, unaware that this is possible, reject both spiritless modern science and the dogmas of organized religion, and then turn to spiritual paths that have come down to us from the Orient. According to Steiner, however, Eastern disciplines such as controlling the breath initially were developed and practiced at a time when humanity's physical constitution, particularly the brain and nervous system, was quite different from what it has become. To imitate such practices today therefore "violates our constitution."

Another apparent path to the spirit that has recently gained notoriety is mediumism or chanelling. Whereas spiritual science requires the rigorous schooling of thinking, feeling, and willing before one can find one's way into the spiritual worlds, the medium's or channel's "soul-spiritual being is virtually paralyzed and put to sleep for a time, so that his or her body, which is of course always connected with a spiritual element, functions automatically." Steiner calls mediumism "a lazy person's approach to the spirit."

Such is not the case with anthroposophy which aims, as we have said, at a conscious transformation of the inner life, one that can bring about a constructive, positive change in outer public or social life. For example, public life is permeated with empty, meaningless phrases. Statements made, for instance, by individuals campaigning for public office often have little connection to reality. Empty talk, that easily slips into lying, is passively heard, accepted, and eventually forgotten by the public. According to Steiner, it is through the influence of natural science, which focuses exclusively on physical matter, that present-day languages have become "emptied of meaning." Concepts derived from natural science permeate our language and make it useless for understanding human relations and institutions. In these lectures the case is made that, through the anthroposophical worldview and practice—which take into consideration the whole human being (body, soul, and spirit)—words will be filled with meaning again, because they will be an expression of the spiritual nature of the human being and the world as revealed to us by a genuine spiritual science.

Steiner points out that empty phrases have a crippling effect on our political life. Instead of rights and laws being a reflection of the living relation between people, they degenerate into outer conformity or convention. And in the economic sphere, empty phrases provide no stimulus for the will to work. Consequently, work is reduced to a humdrum, mechanically performed routine.

Only when words can express the spiritual nature of the human being and the living relations between people will dignity be a part of our political relations and can a new will be found for working in our economy.

In conclusion, I would like to draw the reader's attention to one of the most radical social demands of the twentieth century: the complete liberation of cultural life from governmental and economic control. This is referred to in these lectures and developed more fully in *Towards Social Renewal*. This means not only the separation of church and state but a separation of the state from everything having to do with individual development, including the field of education. There is no premise more tenaciously clung to by every modern form of government than the belief that the state should control the content and goals of education. But if true social renewal is to take place, the human spirit must be able to develop out of its own needs and not be subject to the demands of the state or the wishes of the economy.

To some people, this demand may seem to border on anarchy, but such is not the case. Yes, the government would lose the power to govern individual development but, as Steiner explains elsewhere, everything to do with civil rights and protection from criminal acts would remain within the jurisdiction of a democratic government.

To the degree that countries do permit the spirit to develop, we need to strengthen our spiritual capacities to the fullest measure. We need our governments and our businesses to be permeated by the insights of spiritual scientific research and not have our spirit dominated by political and economic interests. These lectures describe how this can be done if enough people will make the effort.

Gary Lamb

15

SOCIAL ISSUES

Gary Lamb has worked in businesses for the past fifteen years and is co-founder and editor of *The Threefold Review,* an independent magazine for the study of social questions in the light of anthroposophy.

Knowledge of the Higher Worlds and Its Attainment, reprinted. (Spring Valley, NY: Anthroposophic Press, 1983).

The Philosophy of Spiritual Activity (The Philosophy of Freedom), (Hudson, NY: Anthroposophic Press, 1986).

Theosophy: An Introduction to the Supersensible Knowledge of the World and the Destination of Man, (Hudson, NY: Anthroposophic Press, 1986).

An Outline of Occult Science, reprinted. (Spring Valley, NY: Anthroposophic Press, 1989)

Towards Social Renewal, (London: Rudolf Steiner Press, 1977).

Methods and Goals
of Spiritual Science

January 5, 1920

PEOPLE SEEING OUR building, known as the Goetheanum, for the first time may well be taken aback by its architectural style and forms.[1] Indeed, they may object to what they see there. And those involved with the building—which houses the School of Spiritual Science, dedicated to serving the cultural and spiritual interests of the future—will fully understand this when objections against it as merely a first provisional attempt in this style are presented without ill will.

However, a question must be considered that is also significant for everything the spiritual movement represented by the Goetheanum intends and strives for. If we merely needed a building somewhere for a certain cultural stream and a certain kind of cultural-spiritual activity, we could have called in this or that architect and some artist or other and told them what purposes the building was to serve.[2] They would then have built the home for our spiritual scientific activities in a particular style, perhaps in a traditional, a Renaissance, or even modern style. In that case,

17

the relationship between the forms of the building, both on the outside and on the inside, and the cultural-spiritual activity to which it was to be dedicated, would have been only superficial.

Our spiritual movement could not proceed in this customary way. We had to create an outer sheath that harmonized in its entirety as well as in the smallest detail completely with the thinking, feeling, and willing of the cultural-spiritual movement for which it was built. For us, this was a matter of expressing our intentions everywhere in the building's outer forms, even down to the last details. The forms were to be like words or other things we use to express the content of our movement. Therefore we could not make use of some already existing style or forms handed down through tradition. The visible architecture had to be drawn from the same spiritual source from which we derive the content of our world view. The innermost impulses of our spiritual scientific movement, which is also called anthroposophy, as well as the way it perceives its tasks, methods, and goals in view of the tremendous challenges today's civilized world presents, make this a necessity.

Our movement does not want to provide some hackneyed theory or a science that appeals only to the intellect; its purpose is not to serve only a one-sided satisfaction of the longings of the human soul. Instead, while striving to fully satisfy the longings of the soul for a world view, our movement also works on grounding this world view firmly in reality so that it can directly affect our practical, everyday life. Thus, what we have been able to accomplish so far, namely, the creation of architectural and artistic forms appropriate to our cause, is significant for the movement as a whole. Here, our spiritual movement has shaped practical reality directly, though in a relatively limited sphere seemingly remote from daily life. Similarly, it wants to present methods and establish goals that will shape all social and ethical aspects of our life—in short, our society in the broadest sense of the word.

People who build on the foundation of spiritual science should not be unworldly and naive idealists; they are to become idealists who will let their practical, everyday activities be shaped directly by what happens in their soul. Thoughts that so often remain separate and estranged from the rest of our lives must be brought into harmony with the innermost strivings of our soul. The activities of practical, everyday life are to become one with our striving for ethical impulses, for the development of our social impulses, and for religious devotion. Of course, with this outlook and such goals spiritual science has moved far away from what most educated people nowadays strive for and consider to be the right thing.

This must necessarily be so, but it is also necessary that a spiritual movement such as ours finds its way into our civilization, as we will understand when we consider how our modern life developed out of the coming together of very different cultural streams. Today I would like talk about the two most important streams.

Our cultural-spiritual education is the soil in which our religious convictions and moral ideals as well as our whole higher cultural-spiritual life are rooted. Through education people are to acquire capacities and strengths beyond those needed for working with their hands. Besides that, there is our life of practical activities, which has received such intensive stimulation in recent centuries. We are surrounded by a technology inspired by science that has had a profound impact on our social conditions and community life. This technology has transformed modern civilization in a way that would have been inconceivable to people of eight or nine centuries ago.

Let us now consider the origin and development of our cultural-spiritual education on the one hand, which not only dominates higher education but also makes itself felt in elementary schools, and our life of practical activities, which is governed to a large extent by technology, on the other. The answer we arrive at is one that people nowadays have not yet come to terms with. As we will discuss in more detail in our third lecture, we need only look at the foundation of our western civilization, particularly that of its higher, spiritual part—namely, Christianity. Even a consideration of Christianity in the broadest sense and a merely superficial historical understanding will lead us to the realization that we have to follow the route Christianity took as it spread from east to west if we want to find the source of our Christian views and convictions. The latter have shaped so many of our general cultural ideas and concepts to a much larger extent than people are willing to admit. If we trace back our culture along this path, we will find that its origins extend past the Roman and Greek civilizations, a heritage of which our cultural-spiritual education still bears the marks. Ultimately, we will find that the particular inner makeup and spiritual conditions that prevailed in the Orient thousands of years ago in prehistoric times are the source of our cultural-spiritual education, especially in its inner, soul-spiritual aspects.

It is only because this education and culture and inner world view have undergone so many changes over time that we no longer notice that they derive from what originated in pre-Christian millennia out of a spiritual orientation that is completely foreign to modern, civilized life. To understand this long development, it is not enough to consult the documents and evidence the historians offer us; we must go beyond them to prehistoric times. This is very difficult for people of our time because they are convinced that it is only in recent centuries, indeed perhaps only in the last one, that "we have made such great progress" in the cultural, intellectual, and spiritual realm. They dismiss as childish and primitive anything achieved in the earlier times I mentioned.

Individuals free of this prejudice and capable of understanding the prehistoric cultures of the East will realize that they were essentially different from ours but nevertheless were able to offer human souls a rich spiritual content. This spiritual content was acquired in a way completely different from how people nowadays learn what is taught in secondary schools as higher cultural-spiritual education.

In the ancient Orient, people who were to acquire higher spiritual education were selected by those in charge of the educational centers concerned and then had to undergo a total transformation of their being. I am talking here about the educational centers of the Orient of which our spiritual science has direct knowledge. Still, anyone who is unprejudiced and courageous in thinking can infer what happened in prehistoric times on the basis of what has been handed down through history. In those ancient centers elements that are completely separate in our time were still inwardly unified.

These ancient centers, from which everything we bear within us—though in a different form—is derived, were at the same time church, school, and art academy. Art, science, and religion were not separate and distinct but unified in ancient civilizations. People who were to be admitted to the ancient educational centers had to develop their humanity to the full. They had to transform themselves completely and develop a way of thinking different from the one used in everyday life. They had to practice meditative thinking and get used to treating thinking as we ordinarily treat the outer world. In addition, they also had to transform their feelings and will.

It is difficult for us to have a clear idea of what people were striving for back then, for how do we actually view our life? We admit readily enough that children need to develop. The capacities and forces present in children in rudimentary form must be developed in the course of their upbringing. Well, children obviously cannot do this by themselves, and so adults believe they have to educate children to help them unfold their talents and abilities. In the process, they also change the nature of the thinking, feeling, and willing the children were born with. However, to expect people to continue their development after they have a will of their own and have outgrown the education provided by others is considered an imposition. After all, people generally believe that we need to be educated only so long as we cannot direct our development ourselves. As soon as people reach a certain freedom where their own education is concerned, they abandon any further development.

This is the intellectual arrogance prevalent today. People think that as soon as they are able to take their development into their own hands, they are actually already finished with it and are fully developed, mature human beings. This attitude did not exist in the ancient cultures I am describing here. Back then, people continued their education to ever further stages. When children are able to understand, feel, and accomplish something after undergoing a certain training, they experience a kind of awakening in their soul. Similarly, there is also a kind of awakening for adults when they undertake their own further development.

The students in the Oriental mystery centers were schooled for such an awakening on a level of soul activity that was higher than the ordinary one just as the capacities of adults are comparatively superior to those of children. People at that time believed that only those who had undergone such an awakening in adult life were competent to form an opinion about the ultimate and highest concerns of life. The goal of this education was not simply to help the students develop their thinking, feeling, and sensitivity so that knowledge of their connection to a spiritual world would satisfy them. No, in addition to enabling the students to form a world view, their education was intended to develop their capacities for directing the outer, practical, and social concerns of their community. All aspects of life were influenced by this cultural-spiritual training and development.

It is hard for us to fully understand what prevailed in the Orient thousands of years ago, at the starting point of modern history. Our outlook and way of thinking have become very different in the course of evolution, and we have come to think and feel quite differently about life. In ancient times, people who underwent spiritual schooling as outlined here progressed as a matter of course—instinctively, so to speak—to a transformation of their being. Their instincts were different from ours and predisposed them to a vision of spiritual life after a certain transformation. Those who had not undergone such training were prompted by their instincts to look up to what the others were able to impart to them. In regard to their own soul development, people followed the guidance of those trained in the mystery centers, just as they did in the organization of their society, and in their participation in life as a whole.

The instincts that led people to this kind of life have disappeared from our culture just as the soul qualities of the child have been completely transformed in the adult. These instincts and what grew out of the mystery centers together forged an inner orientation in people so that they could not but believe that the essential core of the human being cannot be found in the physical body here on earth. Instead, their whole outlook led people even in their ordinary, general consciousness—instinctively, so to speak—to go beyond the physical to their higher self, something within themselves that was essentially of a soul-spiritual nature. Although it manifests itself in a physical body between birth and death, this higher self is eternal and belongs to the spiritual world, which people back then perceived instinctively.

Though the term has grown somewhat suspect because of the way Nietzsche's followers use it, I would like to say that people in ancient times believed that the true essence of the human being was actually something "superhuman."[3] In other words, people believed that their true nature lay beyond the limits of the ordinary human being. This is what the ancient cultural-spiritual education was very good at: it taught that the true essence of the human being is soul- spiritual and merely comes to expression in the physical body. It enters and directs human life even in its most material aspects from out of the soul-spiritual realm.

The content of this ancient Oriental cultural-spiritual education then went through many metamorphoses and finally arrived in ancient Greece in a form I would like to describe as watered-down. In the earliest period of Greek civilization—the one Friedrich Nietzsche called its "tragic age"—people were still guided toward the higher self.[4] However, in later periods the dialectical, purely intellectual view of the human being predominates. The rich, human, and universal content of the prehistoric cultures was then further and further diluted until it reached our time in an extremely watered-down condition. Thus, our life is also shaped by this cultural stream, which pointed people toward their higher self and gave them an awareness of being a physical manifestation of their soul-spiritual being that was with them at every moment, whether they were praying or working at the most menial task.

In my third lecture we will talk about the Mystery of Golgotha, the starting point of Christianity on earth, as an independent fact that has been understood and interpreted very differently in the course of time. The understanding of this event that is closest to its true meaning was shaped by what had been handed down through ancient Oriental cultural- spiritual education. Basically, a last remnant, albeit spiritually much diluted, of the ancient Oriental outlook survives in everything we do to understand Christianity.

There is a strange fact we have to consider in connection with this inner orientation or outlook, which has survived in us in its final metamorphosis. I am talking about the fact that, grand and impressive as this Oriental civilization was in regard to advancing toward the superhuman, higher self in us, it would never have been able to descend to the level western civilization has reached and where it has achieved its successes. The ancient Oriental cultures culminated in their finding of the superhuman, soul-spiritual essence in us; this was their greatest achievement and they could not achieve anything else.

At the very moment when the Oriental cultural-spiritual life in its final metamorphosis was taking hold in the West, a new cultural-spiritual life was begun here, one that has brought forth enormous benefits for our practical, everyday life. However, these benefits are completely different from those provided by the Oriental spiritual-cultural life I have just described. To begin with, I would like to remind you of something I have already mentioned earlier in a different context, namely, the fact that the customary reference books cite the current population figure of the earth as about fifteen hundred million people. But, strangely enough, when we look at the work that is being done in human civilization, at the people working in the various spheres of life, we arrive at a different figure. For the global amount of work being done does not correspond to the population figure of fifteen hundred million, but points to twenty-two hundred million as the total number of people on earth. For the past three or four centuries, machines have been doing work that we can also picture people doing. We have substituted machine power for human energy. If we convert the output of our machines into terms of human labor, then, based on an eight-hour workday, we get a figure of seven to eight hundred million workers—not actual human beings, of course, but human work that is now done by machines.

This is what the spiritual powers that have developed in the Occident have contributed to our civilization. These spiritual-mental powers could never have developed directly out of the inner soul-spiritual culture that advanced in such a wonderful way to the superhuman or higher self, to the soul-spiritual in human beings. That culture limited itself to certain heights of soul development and did not permeate practical, everyday life as we know it. In that culture, lifeless metals and other materials could never have been put together the way we have done so that now there are not superhuman beings, but subhuman ones, working among us. These "subhuman beings" are actually only homunculi compared to real people of flesh and blood. They are merely mechanisms that contribute to our civilization what we would otherwise have to supply ourselves. This is a typical characteristic of our western cultural-spiritual life, and all the more so the farther west we go. These mechanical, subhuman "beings" are the product of the western cultural-spiritual life, just as the soul-spiritual or superhuman higher self emerged from the ancient cultural-spiritual life in the Orient.

However, this development is not an isolated feature of western civilization. It is closely connected with the development of our thinking, feeling, and willing. The outlook of the creators of these homunculi is impressive and great, though, of course, in a very different way than that of the ancient Oriental people. To understand modern life, we must grasp this contrast in all its intensity. After all, we modern human beings still carry within us the final metamorphosis of the traditions and legacy from the Orient. At the same time, we have absorbed for centuries now the essential element of western cultural-spiritual life, which is completely different. So far, a balance between the two has not yet been established. Rather, the two streams—that of the superhuman, albeit much changed, and that of the subhuman, albeit only in its beginnings—flow alongside each other, unconnected.

When people become aware of these two as yet disconnected streams flowing in their soul, they often suffer psychologically, spiritually, and probably also physically from the resulting discord. True, these things happen at

such deeply subconscious or unconscious levels that what
emerges in our consciousness as well as in our physical
constitution looks quite different from the original cause.
Nowadays people are nervous and dissatisfied with the
way things are. I could list hundreds of other symptoms of
this discord people feel between themselves and the world
and of its effects on their health. The underlying cause for
all this is what I just talked about, namely, the big question
of how we can reconcile for future civilizations the stream
that has produced the subhuman with the one that lives in
us in its final phase as an inheritance from a civilization
that advanced to the soul-spiritual self.

Spiritual science, or anthroposophy, concerns itself particularly with the forces in our civilization I have just
described. It considers balancing the two contrary streams
of soul forces one of the most significant goals of our time.
Anthroposophy knows how absolutely necessary and
important it is for humanity to find ways to reach this goal.

I have described the cultural-spiritual life of the ancient
Orient as instinctive because it grew out of people's
instincts. We have inherited it but only in an already intel-
lectualized form; it exists in our civilization only in
concepts and in abstract notions. This is because we no
longer have the instincts people in earlier times had. We
can fantasize all we want about human beings needing to
return to naiveté and to their instincts—in a certain sense
such a demand is justified—however, this naiveté would
now manifest itself in a very different way than it did in the
past, and our instincts would now take on a different direction. To demand that we become again like people of past
millennia is like expecting adults to play like children.

No, to satisfy the deepest needs of our soul, we can neither go back to the civilizations of thousands of years ago

nor can we call for *ex oriente lux* without falling into decadence. As western people we must not call for the light to come to us from the Orient. The light that is there now has undergone many metamorphoses, and we must not fall prey to the illusion that the spirituality we can find in the Orient nowadays can influence our civilization in a beneficial way.

Indeed, it was the worst kind of decadence when a theosophical movement appeared in response to the religious and cultural needs of western civilization—of the machine age, which has developed a mechanistic world view that cannot satisfy us—and then turned to the region that can offer us only the decadent remnants of the ancient Oriental cultural-spiritual life. The attempt to incorporate Indian culture now into western theosophy reveals the extent of the contemporary spiritual barrenness. Our civilization lacks creative forces in its own cultural-spiritual life. It could achieve success only in technology but proves itself unable to find its own way into the realm the soul needs if it is to understand our true soul-spiritual essence.

This, by the way, is an all too prevalent trend today. Many who are dissatisfied with modern Christianity try to find out what it was like in earlier times. They want to know what the first Christians did and want to imitate them. These people want to return to the way things were then, as though we had made no progress since then and as though we did not need a new understanding of Christianity. Indeed, we see everywhere the signs of barrenness and lack of creativity. That is not what spiritual science wants; it does not want to borrow anything from ancient cultures or from their modern successors. If you understand the concrete foundations of anthroposophy, you will easily agree with what I have said.

SOCIAL ISSUES

Even in our time, many people in the Orient are still trying to find a way to the spiritual realm by imitating ancient
methods. For example, they try to find their way into the
spiritual through certain breathing exercises. Through
controlling their breathing they want to develop the constitution and outlook leading to the inner powers of
knowing, feeling, and willing with which to enter the spiritual world. It is only in the spiritual realm that the soul-
spiritual self and true self-knowledge can be found. These
contemporary Orientals are still doing what their ances-
tors have been doing for centuries and millennia in
pursuing this path: they descend from the merely intellectual life of the head into their whole being. They know the
inner, organic relationship between our breathing, inhal-
ing and exhaling, and the processes of thinking—I will talk
about this in more detail in the next few days. They also
know that thinking grows, so to speak, out of our breathing, and therefore these modern Orientals want to return
to the root of our thinking, to the process of respiration.
That is why they try to enter the spiritual world by controlling their breathing.

This path is not the right one for us. To imitate it would
be to violate our constitution, which has become completely different. The inner structure of our brain and
nervous system is different from the one that gave birth to
the instinctive spiritual culture of the Orient. If we believed
it was right for us to work on controlling our breathing, we
would deny our intellectual life; we would deny what we
are especially suited for.

To find our way into the spiritual world, we will have
to undergo different kinds of metamorphoses. Instead
of reverting from thinking to physical processes such
as breathing, we must school our thinking. That is why

spiritual science, if it is properly attuned to our time, must speak of developing intellectual life. However, I do not mean the kind of intellectual life almost exclusively known today, for that has dried us up, parched us, and narrowed down our perspective on life. Even though many people complain loudly about one-sided intellectualism, they have not come up with anything that could really overcome it.

Mere concepts, even those derived from serious, conscientious scientific inquiry, leave our soul cold and incapable of finding its way in real life. On the other hand, it has not been possible to guide this intellectual life in a direction that can satisfy us because people want to avoid precisely what spiritual science, as we understand it, considers right for present-day humanity. Upon realizing the dryness, insipidity, and one-sidedness of intellectualism, people cannot simply draw emotions out of some kind of a preintellectual, primitive, elemental realm to improve themselves as intellectual beings. After all, in this wild element that we do not understand we cannot find something to graft superficially onto our intellectualistic civilization.

Therefore, spiritual science seeks what modern people need to truly satisfy their soul by developing the soul through various exercises. In the second section of my *An Outline of Occult Science* and in my book *Knowledge of the Higher Worlds and Its Attainment*, as well as in my other writings, I have described in more detail how we should follow this path in a way appropriate to us as western people.[5] Basically, I only want to point out here that this requires that we control our soul life and avoid developing the loftiest concepts and ideas—that is, we must avoid developing one-sidedly only our thinking.

Instead, we have to exercise our soul that the most vivid feelings will accompany our thoughts as they come and go. One-sided intellectuals have a dry and barren thought life; at the same time, they allow their thoughts to wander at will into the field of science, which is so remote from true life, or they otherwise thoughtlessly live for the day. In contrast, the exercises of spiritual science strive to concentrate and deepen our thinking and to develop feelings in this concentration so that we can hate or love, can be glad or angry about what we think just as we can hate and love people and can get angry at outer events. Thus, a whole new inner life is to unfold that is just as vivid and animated as our outer life. The books I just mentioned bear witness to the fact that this can be done systematically.

We will find our way into the spiritual world if we follow this path and develop the forces of thinking, feeling, and willing that are usually dormant within us. We must not start with the body, as the ancient Oriental cultures did, and try to control our breathing. Instead, we have to guide our development through our soul and spirit. And what are the forces we apply in this process? Why, the very ones that have made our modern civilization so successful—the same forces that were used in designing and building machines and in developing the mechanistic, astronomical theories of Copernicus, Galileo, and Newton.[6] In other words, we will develop precisely the keen perception and imagination we used in inventing machines as well as in our astronomy, chemistry, and in our social conditions and community life. The people in ancient Oriental cultures did not have this keen perception and imagination, and they could not have developed them. That is why they had to turn to their breathing as a path to gain higher knowledge.

We, on the other hand, have to begin where we start also in our outer, practical life, namely, with the soul and spiritual forces that permeate our mechanistic culture and have produced about seven to eight hundred million specimens of subhuman "beings." In a sense, we have to reach a new Orient—that is, we have to achieve a new perception of the higher self, of the eternal and immortal self in us, out of the most mechanical elements that have proven to be the path to the subhuman for our civilization.

However, people nowadays do not like everything that needs to contribute to modern civilization. They demand that children be educated, since the latter are too young to make decisions about their own education, but as soon as people are old enough to decide for themselves, they want nothing more to do with further development and education. They consider themselves finished and mature persons and run for office in town councils and parliaments, convinced they already know everything. People think they do not need to stoop to developing the capacities through which they gain knowledge. On the contrary, they feel themselves entitled to be critical of everything once they have become aware of their own will and have come of age so that other people can no longer meddle with their education. Still, modern people need to look for a way to ascend to the heights where they can find their soul-spiritual self.

It is true that at first the inner motivation needed to pursue this path to such knowledge demands sacrifices. This path requires a life full of pain and suffering, a life not everyone has to lead nowadays, and that not everyone is able to endure. We do not all have to become chemists for the findings of chemistry to be useful for us, and we do not all have to be astronomers to benefit from the findings of astronomy. By the same token, there need only be a few spiritual researchers, and yet everyone can understand the results of their research with ordinary, sound common sense, as I have said repeatedly. The relatively small number of spiritual researchers can impart their spiritual insights to others, and all people with sound common sense will understand them.

But that is exactly what many people deny. They take the reports of the spiritual researcher as nothing more than beautiful fantasies and proceed to dissect and analyze them logically. They refuse to accept these insights because to their common sense they are not self-evident. These people usually admit that they have not yet trained themselves to develop their capacities for higher knowledge.

In connection with these rejections we can come across strange things. Just recently another brochure was published about the anthroposophical world view I am advocating. Its author, a "university professor," pulls me to pieces both as philosopher and as theosophist.[7] He claims that I said one has to be a chemist to understand chemistry and a physicist to understand physics—and he agrees with me there. However, he thinks it is strange that I said that we can agree on what the chemists and physicists are saying because, after we become chemists or physicists ourselves, we will clearly see that they were right, but according to this professor I have explained that we have to develop special capacities to understand and verify what spiritual science is teaching. And indeed, that is what I am saying. We have to undergo training as chemists to judge the findings of chemistry or become physicists to evaluate the results of physics. By the same token, we have to become spiritual researchers to assess the insights of spiritual science.

Now, this peculiar professor—well, maybe he is not all that peculiar—goes on to say that it is not a question of my teachings being confirmed by people trained in spiritual science, but of my teachings standing up under the scrutiny of *this* professor. In other words, I am supposed to justify and prove my findings to somebody who not only has not the slightest idea of spiritual science but also does not want to learn about it. What this man has is, of course, the kind of "common sense" that has to be put in quotation marks and is of no use at all in understanding what spiritual science teaches.

However, unprejudiced people with sound common sense can understand it. It may well be that in the future people will think about these things very differently than many do now.

Philosophers have always argued about the world. Surely they must have sound common sense, and if we are unbiased, we can even say that philosophy is better than its reputation. Yet philosophers are always arguing with each other. If we are objective, we can even grant that philosophers have a certain astuteness when they contradict what someone else has said, also based on a certain perspicacity. Now, if we look at this with an open mind, we get a very strange insight into common sense. This common sense does, in fact, exist, and when people talk, they generally do so on the basis of their common sense. However, it is obviously not suited for an understanding of the world; otherwise the philosophers would not have to argue. Ordinary common sense does not seem suited to help us understand the world as our senses perceive it.

Now, we can try to see whether our common sense can understand what spiritual science teaches us—we will see that we will comprehend it. To say that spiritual researchers

35

claim different things, one this and the other that, is worse than prejudice; it is just a load of drivel. People who say such things speak out of ignorance; once they come to know the facts, they will no longer make such statements.

Many prejudices and preconceived ideas will have to be overcome before spiritual science can take its rightful place in modern life. Nevertheless, it will have to gain its proper place, because a way must be found to connect the two streams I have described. We cannot be reactionary and revert to earlier cultural-spiritual forms. Instead, we must take our place among the achievements of the natural sciences and of our mechanistic age. We must spiritualize the forces that inspired people like Copernicus, Galileo, Giordano Bruno, Röntgen, and Becquerel so that we achieve knowledge of our soul-spiritual self through the same soul forces we used to build machines.[8] Then we will no longer just talk about spirit but will be able to fill our striving for the spirit with true substance.

Careful observers of modern civilization are upset by people talking a lot about spirit while being unable to give their talk any substance. As a result, we have world views that are completely unrelated to our practical, everyday life. This is the same as housing our spiritual science and its world view in an old-fashioned building. Our spiritual scientific world view needs to live in a building whose architectural forms have grown out of this world view. Spiritual science is intended and able to work in such a way that it will shape outer material life even in its technical details and in its social relationships. Then spiritual science will become the bearer of a civilization that will find the right way to the goals we have talked about today. Spiritual science will prevent the spreading of the belief that a striving for the spirit implies a demand that people working in factories, for example, must not only do their job there but also have time to devote themselves to spiritual goals. This is not what spiritual science demands. It does not expect people to find their cultural-spiritual life when they have done their work and closed the factory doors behind them. No, spiritual science calls for the opposite: It demands that when people enter the factory to do their job, they should bring in the spirit. They should permeate every machine with the same spirit that will also take our world view to the highest levels of knowledge, to that of the immortal. Anthroposophy does not want more time left free for spiritual pursuits; it works toward imbuing every moment of people's lives with true spiritual substance.

Many people these days are clamoring for the spirit. The other day a book on socialism by professor Robert Wilbrandt from the university in Tübingen was published.[9] It contains a number of sensible and insightful opinions. The book concludes with the professor's realization that we will not get further with socialism if we do not discover the new spirit, the new soul, we need. So here, on the last pages of the book, we find the call for spirit and soul. However, if we lead people like this professor to where the spiritual is filled with content—that is, if we no longer speak only in abstract terms of spirit and soul but talk about the content of soul and spirit in the same way as scientists speak about nature—then such people, lacking the courage to commit themselves to truly content-filled spirit, slink away.

Many people are like that; they cry out for the spirit, but when the spirit requires a real content, they disappear. They stop at merely suggesting some abstract connection between the human soul and the spiritual realm. Our anthroposophical spiritual science, however, has set itself the task of finding a true spiritual content, a true spiritual world, by using our own organic powers of perception and cognition. Anthroposophy wants to unify the two streams of Orientalism and Occidentalism that are now living in us separately side by side. Just as the resulting unified striving has led us down into a mechanistic world, so it can also lead us to the loftiest heights of spirituality.

In conclusion, I just want to add the following comments to this introduction to our theme. In the next two lectures, we will talk about it in more detail than we could today. The call for a new spirituality stirs in the hearts and minds of many. I think we are beginning to see that the tragedy that has hit us so terribly in the last five years is connected with the fact that our spirit has reached a dead end. We can sense that we have to break through a wall to make progress spiritually, that we need new spiritual impulses to advance in society, in politics as well as in technology.

Well, as you know, many generals and statesmen are writing their war memoirs these days. A man who may not always have played a favorable role in recent years, though perhaps a more sensible one than other so-called statesmen, has also just published his memoirs. His book ends as follows:

> The war continues, albeit in a different form. I am convinced that future generations will call the tremendous drama of the last five years a world revolution, rather than a world war.[10]

These are the words of the Austrian statesman Czernin. So there is at least one person who realizes, though only to a limited extent, how things are connected. He continues:

[Future generations] will realize that the world war was only the beginning of a world revolution. Neither Versailles nor St. Germain will create a lasting peace; for this peace already contains the destructive seed of death. The convulsions shaking Europe have not yet diminished. As in the case of a tremendous earthquake, subterranean rumblings continue to be heard. The earth will open up again and again here and there, belching forth fire into the skies. Events of an elemental force will continue to devastate the nations until everything that recalls the madness of this war and the French peace settlements has been swept away.

Slowly and in indescribable torment, a new world will be born. Future generations will look back on our time as on a long nightmare. But even after the darkest night a new day always dawns. Entire generations have sunk into the grave, victims of murder, illness, and starvation. Millions died in the effort to kill and destroy, with hatred and murder in their hearts.

But new generations will be born and with them a new spirit. They will rebuild what war and revolutions have destroyed. Every winter is followed by a spring. It is an eternal law that in the cycle of life, death is followed by resurrection.

Happy are those who will be called as soldiers, not to fight, but to work and help build the new world.

Here, out of the limited understanding of an old-style politician, we hear again the call for a new spirit, which has to be understood and to take root in our soul. After all, even the most external things in life are connected with its most inward aspects, the most material events with the most inward spiritual experiences. When we look at how the spirit that had its heyday at the beginning of this century expressed itself in the events of recent years, we realize that the call for a new spirit had to come. In its methods and goals, anthroposophy wants to be closely connected with this new cultural-spiritual life in building a new world, just as the spiritual movements that oppose ours have evidently been linked to the terrible events of recent years.

A few days ago, I read a strange lecture, given in the Baltic region. Its date—please take note of this—was May 1, 1918, and it was given by a physicist.[11] He concluded by saying that the world war has certainly demonstrated that the various scientific, cultural, and spiritual efforts of the present time are much too isolated from each other. According to this physicist, the war taught us that in the future the work done in science laboratories must be organically connected with the work of the general staff of the armed forces. There has to be constant exchange of ideas between the two. Indeed, this physicist said we must strive for a close alliance between science and the armed forces— in this alone, according to him, lies the salvation of the future.

As we can see here, scientists of the old guard actually consider a pact between themselves and the most destructive forces of humanity an ideal to strive for. Anthroposophy, with its spiritual striving, on the other hand, wants to enter into an alliance with all truly constructive powers in human civilization.

The Foundation of Physical and Mental Health in Spiritual Science

January 6, 1920

My talk yesterday was an introduction of the methods and goals of spiritual science, and tomorrow we will discuss the important consequences of this spiritual science that affect the concerns of the present time as well as our ethical, social, and religious forces. But today I would like to insert a discussion of what spiritual science has to say concerning our physical and mental health. Talking about this topic is justified because, after all, we can set ourselves ethical and social goals worthy of a human being, and develop a religious life out of the depths of our soul, only when our goals and activities grow out of a healthy body, soul, and spirit.

As you will probably expect from an anthroposophical discussion of health, we will focus especially on the spiritual and psychological factors involved. In talking about this topic, we immediately come up against one of the oldest controversial questions, namely, the one about the connection between the soul-spiritual and the physical parts of our being. Much has been thought about this question, and much research has been done in various sciences to clarify and understand the relationship between our soul-spiritual element and the physical body.

The spiritual science we are talking about here, however, has to adopt the standpoint that this question as it is usually phrased is not really put in the right way. People usually ask how our soul and spirit relate to our physical organization. They do not take into consideration the possibility that the soul constitution and capabilities over which we have some control through our will power create a special relationship between spirit and body in certain people. In other words, people do not consider whether it is possible that we can affect our physical organization with the forces we develop in our soul. To deal with this question properly we need the kind of spiritual scientific inquiry I introduced to you yesterday.

After all, when we consider what made western science, as I have described it yesterday, so successful, we have to realize that it was not a quality that leads us to a deeper understanding of the human being, but rather one that takes us farther and farther away from it. What are the goals that those scientists who have accepted the principles of the last three or four centuries strive to accomplish for their field of science? Their goal is to develop concepts of the things around us and of the human being that are as much as possible, perhaps even completely, free of any human emotions or will impulses. The more the subjective, personal elements can be excluded from scientific inquiry, the closer these scientists believe they have come to achieving the ideal of scientific research. Physicists and biologists nowadays think they are not fulfilling their duty if they include in their findings anything that can be understood only in the soul.

Now, let us recall the ideal of the ancient Oriental world view that I described yesterday. There the human being as a whole was involved in the transformation and development of human nature that was the foundation of the Oriental world view. The oriental method thus is the exact opposite of what is now considered the scientific ideal we need to strive for. In dealing with these things, we have to cast off many preconceptions that are still accepted as self-evident truths. However, they will soon be exposed as prejudices that developed out of the way people have been educated over the past three or four centuries.

A closer look at the nature of our way of thinking, shaped and permeated by science, reveals that it acknowledges only one part of our being, namely, the intellect. The thinking of the intellect is not influenced by our emotions or our will; the intellect tries hard to avoid adding anything of a subjective or personal nature to the process of thinking. Consequently, we do not participate in the most important work of science with our whole being; only that part of us, the bearer of the intellectual soul life, is involved.

The true western striving for a spiritual scientific outlook I described yesterday does not revert to ancient Oriental ideals, but aims to develop out of our whole being the soul forces needed to create a world view. Yesterday I characterized the path leading to a spiritual scientific world view as follows. While scientists develop intellectual concepts by experimenting and observing nature, we have to draw purified feelings and impulses of will out of the depths of our soul if we want to arrive at a spiritual scientific world view. Of course, we too have to immerse

ourselves in our thoughts and be able to work on an intellectual level equal to that of the most exact scientist.

However, the relationship of our whole being to our
intellectuality is different from that of the scientist. We also
delve into the world of ideas, the world usually seen as one
of pale and shadowy thoughts, but our feeling and willing,
our sympathies and antipathies, which we usually reserve
for events and challenges in outer life, now also accompany our thoughts and ideas. Our ideas, their effects and
interrelationships, now evoke sympathy or antipathy and
the activity of our will, all of which we usually use only to
respond to fellow human beings or to nature, to pangs of
hunger or thirst, or to the tasks of our everyday life. The
methods leading to spiritual scientific insights make us as
alive and active inwardly as we are in our willing when we
are hungry or thirsty or as we are in our emotions when we
are stirred by love or hatred for other people. We are
involved in these methods with our whole being, including our feelings and our will. As a result, we develop quite
different insights and quite different relationships to the
world and to other people than purely intellectual efforts
can give us.

Unfortunately, spiritual science is still a closed book for
the great majority of people today—not because spiritual
scientists have closed and sealed the book, but because
people prefer to close it with their prejudices, scorn, and
derision to avoid actually having to examine its contents.
Still, when people take up the teachings of spiritual science
and unite them with their whole soul, the effect of our
teachings will be quite different from that of merely intellectual knowledge. The contents and substance of spiritual
science directly engage our whole soul, filling it with
strength and energy. When this content has been acquired

according to cosmic laws and relationships, it will pour the same forces that build up our organism into our soul. For our body is built up out of cosmic forces, and the methods of spiritual science lead us back to those forces. Therefore, there has to be an inner harmony between what spiritual science teaches us about the laws of the universe and the organization of our physical being because the latter is determined by the foundations of the cosmic order.

As a result, the relationship between the content of spiritual science and our development is quite different from the relationship we have to something that addresses only our intellect, such as the natural sciences or modern social science. However, this relationship is not readily perceptible, and this makes it difficult for people who have not yet penetrated to the deeper meaning of spiritual science to get a clear picture of these things. We need to emphasize therefore that the healthy human being is organized out of the cosmos in a natural, wholesome way. And the insights of spiritual science, when they are acquired in a sound and healthy way, will encompass our whole being and therefore can act not only on our intellect but on our whole being.

Newcomers to spiritual science may grant us, hypothetically at first, that we derive healthy thoughts from our spiritual scientific investigation of the world. They will admit that intellectualistic and shadowy thoughts will not have any effect on our organism. But since our thoughts have been conceived out of our whole being, they can act on the human organism. Thus, these people may grant us, at least hypothetically, that these thoughts can be applied in accordance with healthy human nature. These newcomers may then agree to use the healthy thoughts we have developed in our spiritual science. They may fill themselves with these thoughts, letting them work on

45

themselves as a remedy to offset their deviating from their healthy human nature. Although this is a plausible hypothesis and is widely believed among certain superstitious people, it has little to do with reality, at least in the way I have phrased it just now.

At this point it is necessary to touch briefly on the foundations we have to establish so that we can properly understand the relationship between a healthy body and a healthy soul and spirit. At birth, or at conception, when we enter this physical existence from the spiritual worlds, we clothe ourselves in a physical body. As we know, it takes time for the soul-spiritual element cloaked in the physical body to make itself felt. Children are born with certain capacities and a certain potential, but they still have to develop. As we watch them grow up over the years and decades, we can see the potential inherent in their soul-spiritual being manifesting itself gradually in their physical organization. The spiritual science we are talking about here will make it possible for us to understand the true connection between the physical and the soul-spiritual spheres. This will lead us to the following insight, not through some logical fantasy, but on the basis of thorough, conscientious observation of life over a long period of time. We will realize that just as it takes time for our soul-spiritual being to become integrated into our physical organization, so everything we take in through our soul and spirit needs time to become embodied in our physical organization.

For example, when I take in a certain soul-spiritual insight at the age of eight, or twenty, or even fifty, this content that stirs my soul is, in relation to my body, as young when it enters my soul as the soul of a child is compared to its body. It will take time before this soul-spiritual insight will make itself felt in my body. Therefore, we cannot hope to come up with thoughts we can administer to people like drops of medicine—this is done in American mental healing—with the expectation that they will produce instant results. No, in permeating the physical body more and more, the soul-spiritual insight undergoes a transformation, and this takes time. Though the time needed varies depending on the spiritual contents, a certain time interval always separates the moment when we take in a soul- spiritual insight abstractly and understand it from the time when it has finally completely shaped our organization.

What I am telling you here is not just some idea or other that can casually be derived from the phenomena of life. It is the outcome of research that is every bit as thorough and conscientious as that done in any laboratory or clinic—in fact, even more so. This research starts with the paths of ordinary human perception, particularly with our ability to call up from the depths of our soul, as if by magic, what we have at one time perceived and stored there. Most people completely ignore what happens in our soul when we remember something. They do not notice, for example, the great difference our soul feels between recalling something that happened decades ago and an event that occurred just three days ago. True, we call up both memories from the depths of our soul. However, what we experienced just three days ago, or even as much as three years ago, comes up from shallower depths of the soul, so to speak, as will be clear to anyone able to observe such things. These memories are still part of the current contents of our soul. In contrast, distant childhood memories we recall in our later years obviously come from far greater depths, and when we look at this process more closely, we realize that this memory from our earlier years is closely interwoven with our body. It permeates our physical organization as though it were blood. The remembered experience has already taken on the character of the forces that make up our habits.

This is of course only a sketch of the much more detailed method for observing how the soul-spiritual insight we take in becomes integrated into our organism over time. This explains why spiritual science has to insist that its way of cultivating our physical and psychological health must not be ranked among the approaches claiming immediate results. Rather, it has to work on the education of our children, on our national education and national life. In other words, spiritual science must work for the health and well-being of humanity with an eye to the future, prophetically, so to speak.

To understand what I have outlined here is to realize what it means to let the impulses of spiritual science enter into our educational methods, to be motivated by spiritual science in bringing up our children. What the children are taught will be permeated not with spiritual scientific theories—there is no need to fear that—but with the anthroposophical outlook and spirit and, above all, with the fire of pedagogical enthusiasm based on spiritual science. Then we can plant in the children's soul the seed of what is later to unite with their psychological and physical organization. This seed is to grow and unfold later, and because it is sound and wholesome, it will become one with their organism in a healthy way, strengthening them, keeping them healthy, and enabling them to resist outside influences.

When the full import of what spiritual science can achieve in this regard is fully realized, then all the beautiful—and I don't mean this word ironically but quite seriously—the beautiful theories about infectious diseases will gradually lose much of their significance though they will perhaps not disappear completely. It will become less important to study how germs and bacteria invade our organism, and instead we will look at whether we are strong enough in soul and spirit to withstand their invasions. This strength cannot be brought about by any external medication, but only through the remedy that strengthens us inwardly in our soul and spirit, namely, a sound and wholesome spiritual scientific insight. Spiritual science thus would put public health care on a very different basis than seems conceivable to people who are convinced that our salvation depends on perpetuating the current outlook and ideas.

I would now like to draw your attention to something I have mentioned here earlier to some people in a different context. Nowadays educators put great emphasis on teaching children through direct perception and experience, and rightly so. For within certain limits it is good to expose children directly to outer or inner perceptions and to let them develop their own ideas and concepts in the process. However, not everything children need in order to be prepared for a life worthy of human beings can be taught in this way. Children will have to learn much simply by looking up to their teacher as an authority figure. Thus, educators have to develop a certain fiery enthusiasm in their teaching so that they can impart imponderables to the children through their fire and passion. Children will learn many things simply because they are convinced that the authority figures they look up to believe these things are important— even though the children may not yet be able to fully understand what they are learning. Fifteen or twenty years later, when they have long since left school, the time may come when they remember as adults something they learned but did not grasp when they were children. But now that they have grown up and matured, they can call up this content as a memory from the depths of their soul and understand it.

If you understand human soul life, you know that comprehending something we have carried in our soul for years, or perhaps even decades, through the process of maturing develops forces in our soul that strengthen us inwardly. Nothing energizes our will as profoundly as much as coming to understand gradually through our own maturing something we had accepted merely on authority many years earlier.

This is how we can combine education with spiritual hygiene. Only when public health care will finally be based on such far-reaching insights, will the spiritual element rooted in the human race actually be able to unfold its health-giving forces. What we take in only through our intellect, in the course of our intellectual development, is in a sense detached from our being and can therefore not really affect us. However, spiritual scientific insights are drawn from our whole being, and therefore they can work on us. If we do not content ourselves with instantaneous and short-lived successes in medicine, but instead develop health care that takes into account cosmic laws, it will be possible for us to achieve immense benefits.

Unfortunately, however, people these days do not want to concern themselves with anything beyond the present moment, with long-range effects and goals. People would prefer to have cosmic laws that allow them to become sick when it is convenient—you know, of course, that I do not mean this literally, but such a tendency is part of human nature—and to be cured again instantly when they want to. However, in our education and throughout the individual's life, we have to aim at developing the inner strength to bring to bear the healing forces in soul and spirit. You see, our physical and psychological health depends on our developing a soul life that is so strong and so full of energy that it can actually work on and shape our physical organism.

To achieve this goal, we need to take longer periods of time into consideration. Events affecting our intellect do not simultaneously work on our will. If we have never worked on our will, and then later in life try to influence our soul by way of the intellect, we will not succeed no matter how hard we try or how sound our ideas and thoughts are. After all, no soul-spiritual content enters the soul directly from the intellect. Clearly, we also have to work on our will. We work on our will through everything that stimulates our interest in the world, everything that arouses our loving sympathy with the world around us. Unfortunately, there are people who go through life with a certain feeblemindedness, so to speak. There are certainly deep reasons underlying this, but one of the causes for this feeblemindedness is that when these individuals were children, the adults around them did not manage to stimulate in them a far-ranging, vivid interest in everything going on in their surroundings. You see, it is this developing of interest that works on the will. Only if the will is strengthened in this way can something that affects the intellect in later life also gain influence on our whole being.

The worst thing that can happen to us regarding our physical and psychological health is for our physical organism to separate from our soul-spiritual being. Such a separation is induced, as though in an experiment, in the trance state connected with mediumism. The medium's soul-spiritual being is virtually paralyzed and put to sleep for a time, so that his or her body, which is of course always connected with a spiritual element, functions automatically. Looked at from the proper point of view, the condition of the medium is actually one of sickness; it indicates a true disharmony between a weakened soul-spiritual element and a predominating physical body. That is why mediumism in its more radical forms is always coupled with a paralysis of the will, or even a paralysis of the medium's whole soul. Since morality can grow only out of our soul energy, we also generally find a certain moral degeneration accompanying mediumism. You see, when we really understand the connection between soul-spiritual and physical health, we realize the drawbacks and negative aspects of mediumism.

People who judge spiritual science without really knowing it unfortunately often confuse it with all the aberrations of our time I have mentioned here. Of course, they find it easier to learn about the spiritual world through mediumism, which is actually insipid, than by studying spiritual science—after all, the latter would require some effort on their part. However, to use a medium is to get descriptions of the spirit from someone whose spirit has been put to sleep. This is a lazy person's approach to the spirit. Our spiritual science, on the other hand, demands not that we put to sleep somebody else's spirit, but that we develop our own inner spiritual capacities to a higher level. Then we can lead our spiritual forces into the supersensible realm to perceive its nature and characteristics. If people considered spiritual science objectively, they would realize that it is the ideal cure-all against aberrations such as the ones I have described here briefly.

Health care, then, is a necessary consequence of the contribution spiritual science wants to make to human development. Of course, people are subject to many different influences, and what I have said should not be interpreted to mean that by pursuing spiritual science we could someday eliminate all diseases. That is not at all what I mean. All diseases have a cause, but knowing how to heal them is more important than identifying their causes. And this is where spiritual science can contribute not only to health care, but also to the field of medicine as well as to practical, everyday life in general.

Many conscientious students of medicine find themselves agonizing bitterly when they are finally let loose on suffering humanity because then they realize how much insight the human organism demands when it has become sick and how little help the methods and teachings of pure natural science are to them. This is true even though many people deny it because they do not want to admit the truth.

The drawbacks of the purely scientific approach reveal themselves particularly clearly in medicine. Of course, this approach also has its advantages where knowledge about outer nature is concerned. Still, in medicine we find the negative aspects of the natural sciences. After all, the chief goal of the natural sciences is, as I said, to completely eliminate the human being from their concepts by looking at the world in a purely intellectual way and by studying natural laws intellectually and through experiments. Through observation, scientists learn as much as can be learned in this way about the effectiveness of this or that remedy or natural product. But they lack an inner understanding of the human being as a whole and of our relationship to nature's products, be they food or remedies. It is only when we proceed in an unbiased and trusting way from mere natural science to medicine that we realize what it really means to eliminate the human being from our methods and then to apply what we have learned to the human organism.

The natural sciences eliminate everything coming from within us in order to, as they claim, achieve objectivity. However, this will take its toll. The sciences achieve objectivity, but at a price: the human being is no longer included in this objective science. First, scientists remove themselves from their investigation—so it is no wonder that the human being is not included in the science they establish. But then the scientists try to apply their findings to human beings. This will prove to be impossible because the human being as such has not been taken into consideration all along.

The exact opposite is done in what anthroposophical spiritual science strives for. Here, the whole person is involved in developing a view of the human being and the world. The results of this spiritual science also have a very different foundation. To clarify what I mean, I would like to remind you again that the spiritual science I am talking about is basically only an elaboration of what began as a new approach to the study of nature developed by the widely unappreciated scholar Goethe.[1] Please note that we are talking about him now as a scientist, not as a poet. We named our building in Dornach *Goetheanum* because we are engaged in Goetheanism. However, what we mean by Goetheanism is not what Goethe scholars mean who think that his spirit ceased working at his death in 1832 and that their only task now is to study what Goethe achieved. Our brand of Goetheanism does not entail going back to his death, but continuing to work in the Goethean spirit now in the year 1920. After all, what was still quite elementary in Goethe's studies can be understood better now from a higher vantage point in human evolution.

Now I want to talk about something that will at first
seem unconnected to our subject, but I will use it to show
how Goethe's approach can lead us to the loftiest heights
of spiritual science. Goethe studied the similarities and
kinships among the beings in nature. He realized that a
plant is really nothing more than a very complicated leaf,
and that each leaf is really a whole plant in itself, albeit a
very simple one. Thus, he was able to see each part of an
organism as the metamorphosis or transformation of the
other parts.

Among other things, he wanted to know how the shape
of our skull bones developed. Like other unprejudiced
observers, Goethe was puzzled by this shape. In his writings, he recounts having visited the Jewish cemetery in
Venice and finding a sheep's skull there that had been split
open. The bones had broken apart in such a way that the
form and arrangement of the pieces made an immediate
impression on Goethe's soul. Looking at the form of the
bones, he realized that the skull bones are nothing more
than transformed or metamorphosed vertebrae. As
Goethe saw it, the skull bones developed when certain
projections of the ringlike bones of the spine became more
pronounced and certain lumps were flattened out. In other
words, through some transformations a simple vertebra
could develop into a skull. Thus Goethe was the first to
state the fact—which has been confirmed by modern anat-
omy after some modification—that the skull bones are
transformed vertebrae.

Allow me to tell you about a personal experience here,
which may clarify what we have been talking about. Since
the late 1870s, I have been deeply interested in Goethe's
views of natural science and have been writing about
them since then. His insight into the metamorphosis of the

vertebrae into the bones of the skull was one of those I elaborated. I had to wonder how a man so universally brilliant as Goethe could have failed to see that the logical next step from this insight is to look at the complicated structure of our brain as a further development of the simple nerves in our spinal cord. Thus, the brain would have to be considered a metamorphosis of the simple nerves in our vertebrae. At the end of the 1880s, when I was asked to work at the Goethe and Schiller Archives in Weimar to help with a first edition of as yet unpublished writings of Goethe, I naturally felt it a welcome task to look for some evidence that Goethe had already arrived at the insight that the brain is developed out of the simple nerve ganglia. And lo and behold, as I opened one of his notebooks dating from the 1790s and filled with his pencil scribblings, I came upon his notes about the development of the brain—just as I had anticipated!

This incident serves to illustrate a way of looking at things that is very different from a purely intellectual study of natural laws. Of course, Goethe's work was only the elementary stage of this approach. This way of seeing things, which came naturally to Goethe as though by instinct, involves the human being as a *whole*. The dissecting, analytical, experimental methods of contemporary science cannot lead us to understand these metamorphoses properly because that requires taking *everything* into consideration, not only what we can count and measure. We also have to consider what we can study only in its intensity or quality. In fact, in spiritual science we have to go still further and actually study things for the characteristics the cosmic spirit and soul have imprinted on them, something we cannot perceive with the methods of conventional science.

With the methods of spiritual science we get results that may sound at first like an aperçu, but they are in fact the outcome of over thirty years of spiritual scientific work. I am referring here to our insight that the human being consists of three members or parts.

People generally assume that our soul and spirit are tied to our sensory nervous system. This is the current, one-sided view. If you know how the sciences developed, you understand that the belief that our inner life depends solely and completely on our nervous system inevitably had to arise. In my book *Von Seelenrätseln*, published two years ago, you can read what I have to say about this on the basis of my spiritual scientific investigations.[2] There I explain that only our intellectual and sensory life—that is, our perception of the world and intellectual processing of these perceptions—rely on the sensory nervous system as a tool. Our emotional life, however, depends directly—not just indirectly—on the rhythmic element in us, that is, on our respiratory system and blood circulation.

Our rhythmic system is connected with the carrier of our intellect in a peculiar way, which can be described as follows. The most important part of our brain is the so-called cerebral fluid. Our brain is indeed first of all an organ of nerves; its task is to process the perceptions of the senses. At the same time, our brain is afloat in this cerebral fluid, which fills our cranial cavity as well as our spinal column. It, too, has a special task to perform. When we exhale, the level of cerebral fluid drops; our diaphragm rises and therefore the cerebral fluid level falls. The opposite happens when we inhale. Thus, our cerebral fluid level rises and falls in a continuous rhythm. This rhythm of rising and falling is the external vehicle of our emotional life. The interaction between the experiences conveyed by the brain nerves and the rhythm of the cerebral fluid leads to an exchange between our thoughts and feelings.

This is an area where the anthroposophical knowledge of the human being will have to work hard and long before we can fully understand our true soul-spiritual and physical being. It is only when we have developed within ourselves the methods described in my books *Knowledge of the Higher Worlds and Its Attainment, An Outline of Occult Science,* and others that we learn—after having created a soul life capable of understanding these things—how to separate our emotional life from our intellect.[3] Otherwise these two are intermingled. The methods of conventional science will not lead us to the realization that our brain and nerve-sense system are only the bearers of the intellect and that our emotional life is carried by our rhythmic system. Similarly, the vehicle of our will is the metabolic system in all its processes, including those in the brain. These three— the sensory nervous activity, the rhythmic system, and the metabolism—comprise the human being as far as physiological functions are concerned. They make up the whole human being.

Spiritual science aims at understanding this whole human being with the help of the powers of cognition of our whole being. Spiritual science can indeed understand the totality of the human being because it relies not only on the intellect but also uses what our emotional life and its carrier, the rhythmic life, have to offer and in addition draws upon what lives spiritually in our metabolism. In this process, spiritual science comes to understand the significance of our lungs, liver, spleen, and of the other organs of the body, for their meaning can only be understood with the help of the spirit permeating everything.

This is how we arrive at an intuitive understanding of the human being and an intuitive medicine. Conceiving of human beings as mechanisms will help us understand only the mechanical aspects of our body but not ourselves in our whole being. Only when we take the Goethean approach, which is an intuitive one, even further and spiritualize it even more will we comprehend our various organs in their metamorphoses. Once we have understood the significance of the metamorphoses in our organism, we can begin to integrate ourselves into nature on the basis of this understanding. However, if we study nature under exclusion of ourselves, we cannot find our place in it. When we really understand ourselves in the way I have described, we can take our proper place in nature. As we study our organism, we realize the deep kinship between ourselves and the cosmos. We will also see the relationship between the food we take out of nature and our organism as a whole. Then we will also understand the relationship between remedies from outer nature, or, as in the case of spiritual healing, from our soul realm, and our whole being.

Today I could only briefly explain this view of the human being, but what I have outlined here is the path that leads from anthroposophical spiritual science to the intuitive medicine many physicians long for who have completed their medical studies and then feel they have been let loose on suffering humanity. They feel that what they learned about the human being and the art of healing lacked the intuitive, spiritual element. Medicine is the most striking example of what happens when science eliminates the human being from its methods.

I know very well that what I am presenting here is still met with a wall of prejudices, but we have to tackle it again and again. It will take a long time before a large number of

people will try the path I have outlined here because it is
indeed less convenient than the one that is usually chosen.
Just as the whole plant is a complicated leaf in the Goethean sense, so we are comprised, so to speak, of three
beings: the thinking human being that perceives the world
through the senses, the rhythmic human being, and the
metabolic one. Each of these functions represents in a sense
a human being, and we have to construct our complete
human nature out of these three members. Each member
has its own unique relationship to outer nature, different
from that of the others. However, the mysterious relationship between illnesses and remedies can be discovered
only by the intuitive medicine I have just described.

I realize that many people consider it presumptuous of
spiritual science to get involved in medical reforms. But it
must do so to fulfill its sacred obligation to the progress of
humanity. Spiritual science cannot help seeing that the
methods the natural sciences have applied so beneficially
over the last three or four centuries to many areas of life
can never be salutary and good for people suffering from
an illness. After all, mere intellectual knowledge of the
laws of aesthetics does not make you an artist. By the same
token, simply knowing the current natural laws does not
make a physician a healer. Instead, physicians have to be
able to live in the activities, the ebb and flow, of nature with
their whole being; they have to be able to immerse themselves completely in creative, weaving nature. Only then
will they be able to follow with sincere, heartfelt interest
the natural processes accompanying illness. At the same
time, studying healthy people in this way will help physicians to understand them when they are ill.

Thus, it is the task of spiritual science to guide us
toward a hygiene developed out of spiritual forces and

also to prepare the ground for an intuitive medicine. Those who embark upon this spiritual science will realize that today I could sketch the path to an intuitive medicine only in broad, general, and rather abstract outlines. They will also see that much of what I have outlined here has already been developed further, waiting only for the moment when the official representatives of medical science come to the realization that these things have to be taken up. This is true for physical as well as for mental illnesses. Nowadays one cannot help appearing presumptuous if one wants to point out what spiritual science can contribute to the welfare and salvation of humanity on the basis of its reliable findings.

I would like to make the transition to what I want to say tomorrow about our ethical, religious, and social nature by saying that spiritual scientists would consider it ideal, especially in regard to the field of intuitive medicine, to have the opportunity to talk with experts in the field. If they are objective and let their expertise guide them, these experts will see how spiritual science can enrich their specialized knowledge. Spiritual science does not fear the criticism of experts; after all, it is not a dilettante movement. Rather, it draws upon scientific sources that run deeper than the conventional science of our day.

If spiritual science had not long since given up being afraid—for obvious reasons—it would be more worried about the laypeople's reaction than that of the experts. Spiritual science has nothing to fear from unprejudiced expertise; for we know that the more objectively and knowledgeably our findings are examined, the more positively will our spiritual science be received.

Envisioning an intuitive approach to medicine brings to mind an old saying, and while I don't want to examine its universal applicability today, I think it is valid in a limited sense for a world view that wants to be useful in the art of healing. This saying from wise people of ancient times is that we understand only what is similar to us. Thus, before we can heal human beings we have to know and understand them. But what is involved in present-day science is not the whole human being, and therefore not the human being at all—not even something like the human being.

It is only when we are involved with our whole being in understanding ourselves that like will come to understand like. This will give us knowledge of the human being and an art of healing that can maintain our health as much as possible in our society and that will at the same time treat illnesses as they can be treated only out of a comprehensive understanding of all healing factors.

Ethical and Religious Forces in the Light of Spiritual Science

January 7, 1920

EVERY WORLD VIEW has to prove its worth by giving people the support they need. This support must include what we might call moral strength as well as the state of soul we get when we feel ourselves a part of the cosmos as a whole, that is, when we feel we are integrated into the world in a way that meets our religious needs. Concerning our inner moral strength, Schopenhauer made quite a poignant comment though the further remarks he added to it can certainly be challenged.[1] He said it is easy to preach morality, but to establish a foundation for it is difficult. How true!

It is indeed relatively easy to realize in general what is good and right and what our ethical standards demand of us; this is a matter of the intellect. However, it is very difficult to summon up from the primeval forces of the soul the motivation we need to participate in life as morally strong human beings, and that is what we mean by establishing a foundation for morality. We lay the foundation for morality not by merely pointing out what is good and right, but by stimulating impulses in people that will develop into

63

true strength and capability within them once they take these impulses into their soul.

Concerning their sense of morality, people nowadays relate to the world in a very peculiar way, which is not always consciously observed but nevertheless causes much of the uncertainty and instability in their life. On the one hand, we have our intellectual knowledge, which enables us to understand natural phenomena, to conceive to a certain extent of the universe as a whole, and to develop a concept of the nature of the human being. This concept, though, is a very limited one, as we have seen in our last two talks. In addition to our capacity for knowing, that is, to everything that is controlled by our logic, another element of our being makes itself felt, namely, the one we draw our ethical duty and ethical love from, in short, our motivation for acting morally. Thus, nowadays we are immersed on the one hand in our capacity for knowing and its results, and, on the other, in our motivations for morality. Both live in our soul, but there is little connection between them—so little, in fact, that Kant could say that the two things he values most highly in all the world are the starry skies above him and the moral law within him.[2]

This Kantian way of thinking that lives in us is unable to find a bridge between our drive for knowledge of the world and our moral impulses. Kant himself treated the two as completely separate; he wrote about the intellect in his book *Critique of Pure Reason* and about the ethical life in his *Critique of Practical Reason*. In all honesty, we have to admit that in our present state of consciousness a chasm separates these two sides of our human nature.

The modern sciences study the evolution of the world and examine all life forms, from the most simple ones and including even inorganic nature all the way up to the human being. Scientists construct theories about the origin of the world directly accessible to our senses, and they even work on hypotheses about how the world as we know it today may come to an end some day. We are an integral part of this natural order, and out of us arise what we call our ethical ideals. These ideals are so important to us that we feel worthy only when we live up to them. In other words, we measure our worth by whether we live in harmony with our ethical ideals. But what will become of our achievement based on our ethical ideals and moral impulses when the whole world as we know it will be brought to its end, as modern science says it will, by natural forces we know or will learn about in the future?

If we are honest and do not cloak our modern consciousness in nebulous phrases, we have to admit that from the point of view of the natural sciences our ethical ideals are indeed what we must live by, but they do not give rise to anything that could survive when the earth, and human beings with it, will be destroyed. We simply have to face the fact that our modern consciousness cannot bridge the chasm between our capacities for knowing, which have brought us knowledge of nature, and the capacities that guide us as ethical beings.

We are not aware of everything that goes on in the depths of our soul; much remains unconscious. Still, what rumbles around in our unconscious makes itself felt in our everyday life in disharmony and in psychological and even physical illnesses. Looking at modern life without preconceived notions, you will realize that life surges all around us, and we are in the midst of it, harboring all kinds of psychological and physical conflicts and discords within us. The life surging up all around us comes from the level of the weak forces that are unable to build a bridge between our moral life and our knowledge about nature.

Spiritual science approaches these issues by leaving behind a merely theoretical view of outer reality. In other words, as I have explained in my last two talks here, spiritual science has to identify and expose all efforts to exclude the human being from this theoretical view of nature for the sake of proper objectivity.

To sum up, let me describe again the path into the spiritual world. First of all, if you want to take this path, you have to devote yourselves to a certain inner, soul-spiritual work or discipline. In my books I called this inner discipline meditation work or concentration work. It will enable you to relate to your thoughts and ideas differently than we usually do when we observe natural or social phenomena. In fact, you will learn to be completely at one with the thoughts that usually accompany our sensory perceptions as mere shadows. As I said, if you seek the path into the spiritual world, you will have to respond to thoughts and ideas with your emotions, your sympathies and antipathies, much as you normally do to people, nature, or other things in the physical world. You have to meet these ideas with your will and emotions just as you would events in everyday life. The thoughts coming to you have to excite you; they have to evoke your sympathies or antipathies and stimulate your life forces. This inner life becomes our destiny, and while we remain outwardly calm, we undergo inner experiences that are no weaker than what we normally experience as our destiny in the outer world. In a sense, then, we are doubling our experience of life.

Ordinarily we get excited, feel sympathy or antipathy, and assert our will forces only in response to external events, but now we have to bring into our thoughts what usually occupies us only in the outer, material world. If we manage to do this—and everybody can do this by doing the exercises I described in my books *Knowledge of the Higher Worlds and Its Attainment* and *An Outline of Occult Science*— then we will come to the point where we not only have mental images of the world when we open our senses to it, but also when we draw solely on our inner, mental life.[3] These images are as full of content and as vivid as the ones we usually have only through our sensory perception. These images are the result of intensifying and strengthening our inner life. Ultimately, then, we become able to live in a world of images that we would ordinarily have only through sense perception and that we can now have without perceiving anything with our senses.

These things can only be understood as we experience them; they are not accessible to abstract logic or so-called proofs. The other important experience connected with this phenomenon is that through such inner work we learn what it means to engage in soul-spiritual activity independent of any physical functions. We will reach a point, paradoxical though it may sound, when we can with good reason admit to being materialists. For then we will realize that in everyday life we are indeed completely dependent on our body as our instrument, and we use the nervous system as our instrument for thinking. It is a distinguishing feature of our outer life that we can describe its scope by saying that we can develop our soul-spiritual being only when it can make use of its bodily instrument. However, our soul-spiritual being does not depend on these physical instruments, but through the exercises I have described it can detach itself from its instruments and become free of the body.

We can speculate and philosophize about materialism as much as we want; yet we will never refute it with what we know from our everyday life. For in terms of everyday life, materialism is right. The only way to refute materialism is through spiritual practice, through separating our soul-spiritual being from our body in our own experience. As a result, we will have mental images separate from our body— of course, by "separate" I do not mean literally outside the body in terms of space, but independent of the body. In my books I have called this whole process imaginative thinking or Imagination. That is one of the things we have to learn in spiritual science in order to build the bridge that, as I have shown, cannot be built any other way.

What we learn in this way with our imaginative thinking is not part of our body, but outside it, and it is the practical proof that our innermost being lived in a soul-spiritual world before entering this body. For in imaginative cognition we are not only outside our body, but also outside the time we inhabit with it. That is how we can really experience the part of us that existed before our birth or, let's say, before our conception. Just as a light from the outside can shine into a room, so in our Imagination our life before birth can shed light into our present life. What shines there into our everyday life is more than mere thoughts; it is filled with a vivid content, which turns out to be something very special, namely, a certain content of our intelligence, so to speak.

By fostering, honing, and strengthening our life of thoughts and ideas in the way I have described, we come to a content of our will that is very much alive. This content of will creates in us something that then clothes itself in the physical body, something we do not receive through heredity or in any other way from the physical world. Thus, spiritual science arrives at the realization of our immortality not through speculatively assimilating what we experience in our daily life, but through cultivating a capacity for knowledge that is usually lacking in our everyday life.

What is especially important for us right now, however, is that in this way we can get beyond our body and even beyond the time dimension in which our body lives. In this process we arrive at ideas that the majority of our contemporaries still find hard to understand; nevertheless, these ideas are an important link in the future evolution of humanity.

When we school not only our life of ideas and thoughts but also our will by practicing our exercises, we make a startling discovery. What I am talking about is that we live pretty much like Faust, who described himself as rushing through life.[4] We, too, rush through life. Granted, we undergo a certain development between birth and death, from month to month, year to year, and decade to decade. Yet, we pretty much leave ourselves at the mercy of outer objective reality.

Honestly now, don't most people just let themselves be carried along by life—first by the adults who bring them up and then by life and fate? They progress and come closer to perfection because the world improves them. Most people just go along with the flow of life. Of course, this does not lead them to the path of spiritual science I have described here. That path requires that we take our development and education into our own hands. It demands that we work on ourselves so that we develop further not just because of what life and destiny bring to us, but because we have decided to adopt a certain outlook. Then we work on making this outlook our own. Whether we undertake such a development on a smaller or larger scale, it makes a big difference that we do something for our own improvement not just because we go along with the flow of life but because we take the development of our self into our own hands. This process teaches us the effectiveness of our will, for we learn what obstacles confront our will when we try to cultivate it for the purpose of self-development.

Indeed, this process is very instructive, and, above all, it strengthens our soul-spiritual forces. After some time of exercising such self-discipline—of course, this takes years of practice—we will find that we gain new inner forces. These forces cannot be found in outer nature nor in the ordinary soul life we had before we began doing the exercises. It is only after embarking upon this path of inner work that we discover these forces, which have a very specific function: they can integrate the moral impulses, which are usually only instinctive, vague, and separate from our capacity for knowledge, into our self in a much more conscious way.

But please don't get me wrong; I am not talking here about the self that lives in our body but about the one we develop only when we go outside our body with our Imagination in the way I described earlier. We cannot integrate the true form of our ethical impulses into our physical body and our sensory perception, but we can incorporate what stands there in isolation—so isolated that Kant distinguished it as the categorical imperative—into our self once it is separated from our body.[5]

Then the Imaginations or inner pictures I described become suffused with the objective power of our moral impulses, with ethical inspiration. As a result, we realize that the ethical imperatives and ideals welling up within us have their source not in us, but in the universe as a whole. Having left our physical nature behind, we also see that these imperatives do not appear in their true form in our physical organization and that their true nature can only be understood through imaginative cognition. We come to understand that these moral imperatives are objective forces in the world.

People can arrive at this insight by weighing with their sound common sense what spiritual scientists are saying on the basis of their understanding of the spiritual world. Once they are imbued by this insight, people will have peculiar feelings when they hear the public talks so popular nowadays. Now, this may sound strange, but I would like to describe what happens as follows. This inspired element in our imagination is congruent with our moral forces, and people who take it in with an open mind and think about how spiritual science really understands these things cannot help but wish that these insights stir people at least as much as the discovery of X rays or of wireless telegraphy did. In view of what sinks down into the soul of the spiritual researcher, we have to admit that it is very necessary for modern civilization to learn to appreciate the powers to strengthen us that can be found on the spiritual path as much as we value what is useful and beneficial in outer life.

I believe that this touches upon an important challenge of contemporary civilization. Let me repeat that spiritual scientific findings are not based on speculation; they are experiences. They are not yet widely accepted because most people allow themselves to be deceived by the materialist outlook of the natural sciences. Their prejudices are the obstacles preventing them from a better understanding because they do not use their common sense. Therefore they cannot properly verify what the spiritual researchers are saying. People are always complaining that they cannot see for themselves what spiritual researchers are talking about. Well, I would just like to know how many of the people who believe in the transit of Venus have ever actually seen one. I would like to know how many people who say that water consists of hydrogen and oxygen ever watched the experiment confirming this—and the list could go on.

But there is, after all, a logic of common sense we can use to put the teachings of spiritual science to the test. I will certainly not be able to deceive people with sound common sense and get them to accept fantastic ideas as real. With their common sense they will be able to tell whether I am talking like a dreamer or whether I am presenting things in a logical and coherent way, basing one idea on the other as it is done in the most precise natural sciences. People who have developed sound common sense will be able to distinguish between a dreamer and a person who can present his views logically and sensibly and who therefore must be taken seriously.

There is much in life we have to decide in this way; why shouldn't we base one of the most important decisions— namely, insight into the cosmic order—on the same process? For those who are not spiritual researchers themselves—and as I have explained in my books, everybody *can* become a spiritual researcher to some extent— there is no other way to verify spiritual science. For spiritual science is a matter of experience; it has to be experienced and cannot be arrived at through logical reasoning alone.

As we come to know world views through this combination of Imagination and an inspired morality, we also learn all about the contradiction between so-called natural causality or necessity and our freedom. For we can live out and express our ethical impulses only in freedom. The view of outer nature that has developed over the last three or four centuries has been shaped by the inevitable connection between an event and the cause preceding it. This is called general causality. All of nature, including human beings, appears to be subject to this absolute or physical necessity. But if this were true, our freedom would be in a bad way, and we would not be able to do anything but what this absolute necessity compels us to do. If the world were indeed as the scientific outlook, which has become popular over the last three or four centuries, sees it, it would not be possible for us to be free.

However, when we have reached the point of being able to observe outside our body, then everything subject to physical necessity appears to us as part of nature's body. This body gives rise to nature's soul and its spirit. In a sense, nature's body has been shed and cast aside by the world in the process of becoming; nature's spirit and soul, on the other hand, will continue to grow into the future. After death, our lifeless body cannot do anything else but comply with the necessities created by the soul-spiritual element that once inhabited it. Similarly, everything corpse-like in nature cannot be motivated by anything other than absolute or physical necessity. Yet, it gives rise everywhere to what will live on into the future. The natural sciences have simply become accustomed to studying only the lifeless body of nature; therefore, they can see only necessity everywhere. That is why spiritual science is needed; it alone is able to see the life that grows and flows everywhere.

Of course, we too are subject to this absolute necessity we find in nature. Yet, at the same time, we also belong to a realm free of causality and filled with an inner experience of freedom. As I described in my book, *The Philosophy of Freedom,* we experience this element of freedom when we advance to an inwardly clear and pure thinking that is actually the product of our will.[6] You will find more details on this subject in my book.

Achieving the capacity to perceive and learn outside of our body leads us into a world where the contradiction between physical necessity and freedom will be comprehensible. We come to know freedom in the world for ourselves and to feel ourselves part of the world where freedom lives.

I am telling you all this not just to give you the contents of what I am saying, but to show you how we can attain a certain condition in our soul when we imbue and quicken ourselves with insights drawn from the realms I have described.

Just as we are filled with gladness on joyous occasions— and just as some people are suffused with a warm glow after several glasses of wine—so our soul as a whole can be completely taken hold of by these real spiritual experiences permeating us. When is our soul stirred by something that approaches it at first only in outer life and only in a shadowy, vague way? Well, every time the categorical imperative or conscience makes itself felt in response to our moral obligations. However, once we work with spiritual science, the contents of our conscience is illuminated and takes on a different shade of feeling. For whether we are ourselves spiritual researchers or have simply accepted, based on our common sense, what the spiritual scientists tell us and have incorporated it into our soul, we have united ourselves with something we can find only when we go outside of ourselves and become alienated from ourselves, so to speak.

Indeed, the best and most realistic definition of love you will ever find is the description of the soul mood that comes over us when we penetrate the essence of the outer world without the help of our body. Whereas we usually experience our ethical imperatives as an obligation, they can be given a form that lets them appear suffused with the same mood that must also imbue the insights of spiritual science. Our ethical imperatives and moral motivations can learn, so to speak, from the soul mood we develop as we take in spiritual science. Our morality can be warmed by what has to live in spiritual science in the highest sense, namely, love.

In my *Philosophy of Freedom*, I explained that the motivation for ethical behavior most worthy of human beings is love. In earlier periods of modern cultural-spiritual development, these things were already talked about in a more instinctive way than the way we will discuss them now that we have made progress—if we wanted to progress, that is—through spiritual science. Kant once spoke of duty and obligation, of the categorical imperative dominating us, so to speak. It does not allow any sympathy to enter in at all. When we act out of moral obligation, we do so because we must. Kant praised duty as majestic and great because it allows nothing charming and flattering, but demands complete submission.[7] Schiller, however, considered this slavish submission not worthy of human beings. He countered Kant's view magnificently and beautifully with his *Letters on the Aesthetic Education*.[8]

We need only look at a brief epigram Schiller wrote in opposition to Kant's rigid concept of duty to see a very different view of morality. Schiller said, "I gladly serve my friends, but unfortunately I do it out of my own inclination. Therefore, it galls me quite often that I am not virtuous."[9] He means that according to Kant we should not

75

be happy serving our friends, but should obediently submit to the dictates of duty. However, life becomes worthy of human beings only when we fulfill what Goethe said so impressively and concisely: duty is to love what we command ourselves to do.[10] The love of what we command ourselves to do can be kindled only out of the state of soul that comes about when we take in spiritual science.

Thus, pursuing spiritual science is not separate from the rest of our life, as preaching morality usually is; rather it leads to a development of forces that directly affect our moral will. Here we find the foundations of morality, for spiritual science fills us with ethical love. It does not simply preach morality, but when it is taken seriously in its full potential, it provides a basis for morality, not through words, but through giving us the strength for virtuous love and for loving virtue. Spiritual science is not merely a theory; it is life. Making it one's own is not just a matter of thinking about it but of taking it in as we take in life in breathing. This is what spiritual science wants to accomplish—and must accomplish—for modern civilization in the area of ethics.

As I pointed out the day before yesterday, a kind of spiritual science existed already in ancient times, but it was of a much more instinctive kind. Where did the spiritual science of the ancient oriental wisdom, which developed millennia ago, come from? It was a dim, dreamlike picturing of the world that grew out of human instincts and impulses; in short, it was an instinctive spiritual science. People at that time could see into nature through a kind of clairvoyance that was connected with their blood and their physical body. At the same time, their morality was also linked to their blood and their body. Both clairvoyance and morality issued from the same source.

As I have stressed here repeatedly, the human race is undergoing an evolution, and to think we could be like the people who lived several thousand years ago is the same as believing adults could be just like children. We can no longer share the viewpoint of the primitive clairvoyance of the ancient Orient or ancient Egypt. We have evolved beyond that through the stages inaugurated by Galileo and Copernicus and have arrived at a way of seeing things that is completely intellectual.[11] In the ancient Oriental philosophy, on the other hand, the intellect was not yet fully developed. As a result of our intellectual development, we now have to draw the motivation for ethical behavior from our spirit and not from our instincts.

One of the worst things people do nowadays is to talk about ideals and motivations in life only in absolute terms. When some party member or some fanatic visionary who wants to set up the thousand-year Reich talks about wanting to achieve this or that goal for humanity, people think that these goals and improvements are good for all people at all times and all over the world. They believe these things are good in an absolute sense. However, out of a true understanding of evolving humanity, we know that what is good and valid according to one world view is so only for a certain epoch. To judge whether something is good for an epoch, we have to know its nature. As I have often said, our anthroposophical spiritual science as I present it does not think of itself as an absolute. It does believe, however, that it speaks out of the heart of the present and the near future and that it is saying to human souls what they need to hear.

At the same time, spiritual science knows only too well that when people will talk about the great cosmic mysteries and the concerns of humanity five hundred years from now, they will do so in a different way, because nothing is absolute and permanent in this realm. It is precisely through being able to see life in its living quality and its metamorphoses even while we are in the midst of it that we are effective.

Of course, it is easier to set up absolute ideals in the abstract than to get to know our epoch and decide what is appropriate for it on the basis of its true nature. But only when we take in the impulses of spiritual science and, as described above, permeate ourselves with what we receive from the spirit can we know ourselves to be spirit and soul. Only then will we know that we live in the world as spirit and soul and see everyone else as spirit and soul. When spiritual science develops thus into an attitude permeating our life, its results will be tremendous. We will consciously encounter other people as riddles we have to solve because we will be aware that in each person we are gazing into infinity, into spiritual depths and chasms.

Our awareness of other people as spirit and soul can develop into social and ethical forces that can then form the foundation for a solution to the urgent social problems of our time. I cannot help thinking that those who fully understand the social problems and the current frame of mind of humanity must be suffering from a certain mental anguish. In our time, the social issues require a particular solution. At the same time, those upholding the social order seem possessed by the most antisocial instincts. The call for a new social structure seems to be in clear contradiction to the antisocial instincts living in the human soul. Regardless of how many beautiful programs we set up and how many beautiful notions we indulge in concerning the solution of our social problems, a way to solve them can be found only when we see, feel, and sense the spirit in people. We have to deal with each other in a way that respects, protects, honors, and loves the spirit and soul in us; in other words, we have to go beyond what people usually believe they meet in their fellow beings.

That is why I have called for a separation of our cultural-spiritual life from the other spheres of our society in my book *Towards Social Renewal.*[12] Then the cultural-spiritual sphere will have a foundation of its own; it can then be guided completely in accordance with the needs and requirements of human nature and be independent of political and economical considerations. It is only through such a free and independent cultural-spiritual life that social impulses and social understanding and attitudes will be spread among people. Our social morality also depends on people taking into their soul what they can gain in studying the teachings of spiritual science. We also need to feel ourselves part of a worthy and dignified whole; we need to feel that we belong to the cosmic whole and are not just lonely wanderers in the world. This feeling, which is the religious element in us, can be kindled and nurtured in the way we need it now only through the mood we develop as we pursue our studies in spiritual science.

The cosmic or historical events to which we respond with our religious feelings are facts. For example, the Mystery of Golgotha is a fact and so is what happened at the beginning of the Christian era in Palestine when Christ incarnated in Jesus. We have to distinguish between these objective facts and people's understanding and interpretation of them. In the first Christian centuries, Christianity found its place in the stream of ideas and beliefs that were passed on from the ancient Orient. Back then, people understood the event of Golgotha with the help of ideas that originated in ancient times, in primeval views of the world. For many centuries, people were honest and sincere in understanding the event of Golgotha on the basis of such ancient ideas.

Then, however, came the time when Galileo inaugurated a new outlook and when Giordano Bruno so remarkably overcame the limits of space in our world view.[13] He showed that the blue firmament above us is only a reflection of what lives in us; it is a boundary of our own making. Beyond it space stretches out to infinity like a vast ocean. Then Copernicus added his insights to this view, and so did others throughout the centuries until now. The result is the modern view of the outer world. In the course of time, people have become used to a view of the world that is quite different from the one through which Christianity was first understood. That is why we now have to develop a new relationship to the religious basis of human history. This is not a matter of disputing the facts on which our religious development is based, but of appealing to people's conscience to enable them to understand the Christ event in a way appropriate to the modern condition of their soul.

To admit that we need to find a new way to understand old facts in the religious realm is to have the most sincere and respectful attitude and intentions concerning religion. Anthroposophical spiritual science is the best preparation for an understanding of Christianity or any other religious idea in a way appropriate to our modern times. To deny this is not to be really sincere and serious about religion; the old ways to understand the foundations of religion can no longer be followed by modern people who have embraced the views of their time.

One of the achievements of the modern age is materialism. Many different kinds of people have been important promoters of materialism, and some of them have pre-served certain older, historical customs. These customs led people to allow the religious denominations to exercise a monopoly in regard to everything concerning soul and spirit. Indeed, because the churches had sole jurisdiction over what people were to believe about spirit and soul, the natural sciences could pursue their researches without taking the spirit into account. The natural sciences now claim that this was necessary, that the spirit must be excluded from an objective study of nature. That is not true; the natural sciences have developed in this way because in earlier times it was forbidden to include the spirit in the study of nature. For back then the churches had the sole authority over soul and spirit. This customary division has been continued to this day and is now even proclaimed as the unprejudiced, objective scientific approach.

We need only look at scientists who rate highest praise in materialistic science, for instance, the Jesuit father Wasmann, who was an expert on ants.[14] He was an excellent materialist natural scientist; he did not let one iota of spirit or religious dogma enter into his work. He kept soul and spirit separate from his research. That is an example for why the conventional, outer sciences are materialistic. Thus, the representatives of the religious denominations have contributed not inconsiderably to the establishment of modern materialism. Paradoxical as it may sound, it is nevertheless true that the natural sciences have lacked the spiritual element because the churches did not allow them to include the spirit in their research. Other sciences followed their example and took up the same habit. Anthroposophical spiritual science, then, must once again carry the spirit into the study of nature.

I would like to repeat here again that, unlike material-ism, spiritual science does not believe it is enough for the spirit to show up for occasional visits to convince people of its existence. No, spiritual science wants to show that in all things big and small, in all matter, there is spirit. We can find the spirit everywhere and at all times. Anthroposoph-ical spiritual science studies the spirit everywhere, even in the most material things, and thus proves that matter does not exist independently of spirit. Just as ice does not exist apart from water but is transformed, frozen water, so mat-ter is spirit solidified. This has to be explained correctly and in detail. By showing that the spirit is at work every-where in matter and in outer life, and by leading people to connect themselves with the spirit, spiritual science pro-vides the impulses for a true deepening of religion.

We can have many interesting experiences in this regard. For example, rather obliging religious people may say that they are unable to verify the spiritual science I present here. They acknowledge that it may contain some truths, but they want it kept completely separate from reli-gion. For religion has nothing to do with knowledge; it is, above all, an immediate relationship, a direct union, between the individual and God. Strangely enough, the people in question then claim that there is already too much religious interest in our time, too many people hav-ing religious experiences or wanting to have them and to develop their interest in religion. Well, according to these religious people, all of this is not necessary in religion; all one needs is the direct union between the individual and God. Therefore, they want to do away with all interest in religion and with all religious experiences.

Well, if we look at this objectively and with an open mind, we will have to say that if people nowadays thirst

vaguely for religious experiences and kindle in themselves
an interest in religion, albeit only a vague one, then this is
the first step toward the yearning to really find a way, such
as I have described just now, into the religious sphere.
Those who are serious about religion should seize this
instinctive interest in religion and religious experiences as
an opportunity. Instead, the clergy frowns upon any interest in religion and religious experiences. One cannot help
wondering who has true understanding for religion, those
who talk like the religious people or those who speak as I
have done here today. Of course, here too we shall know
people by their fruits.

Another person, a theologian who is also a university
professor, recently tried to refute spiritual science in a lecture.[15] Two young friends of mine, who are well versed in
anthroposophy, attended the talk and were able to participate in the ensuing discussion. As the conversation
seemed to call for it, they quoted passages from the Bible
to show that the Scriptures, rightly understood, agree with
what anthroposophical spiritual science is saying on the
same subject. The chairman, a true man of the cloth, was at
a loss what to do and could think of nothing better to say
than "Here Christ was mistaken." To this our friends
replied "So, you believe in a God who makes mistakes?
That's a nice religious persuasion! It surely produces some
odd quirks these days."

Religious feeling is sincere only when it becomes part of
our moral life. Here again strange things can happen. I
have recently found the meanest comments one could pos-
sibly make concerning the social consequences of
anthroposophy in a number of German newspapers.
Those articles were nothing but lies from start to finish;
nevertheless, people think this kind of thing is consistent

with their morals. This is not surprising in a time when the following can happen as the moral result of religious practice. Recently, the canon of a cathedral—that is, a catholic clergyman—gave a lecture on the spiritual science we advocate here.[16] He concluded by recommending that people find out what kind of world view I promote by reading the writings of my opponents because they are not allowed to read my own books or those of my students. The Pope has forbidden Roman Catholics to read those writings. This recommendation to find information about something by reading the most hostile and malicious writings of its opponents is the moral result of many a religious practice of our time. Small wonder then that out of such depths the tragedy we have experienced in the last five years poured forth. Did we not experience there a surfacing of lies and hatred and many other things that had, and still have, their roots in the depths of the human soul? What we have gone through—shouldn't it prompt us to think things over seriously and to ponder a thorough change? After all, what has surfaced in the world at the present time is a kind of worldwide immorality. Or do you think we have seen religious conviction manifest itself throughout the last five years?

Today we can see the fruits of the philosophies and beliefs that had not centuries but millennia to work on the improvement of humanity. Nineteenth-century theology no longer knows anything about the spirituality of the event at Golgotha. This spiritual aspect, the divine Christ in the human person of Jesus can be found again by following the path of anthroposophical spiritual science. From there, Christ will once again find his way into human souls and lead them not to preach morality but to build a foundation for the truly instinctive and impulsive element of moral working and living in the world. Isn't it obvious that such a renewal and rebuilding is necessary? Isn't it obvious when we look at the events of the past five or six years, where we see the fruits of what lived for centuries under the surface and has now come up to it? This should be sufficient proof for the necessity of thorough religious and moral work.

Spiritual science wants to participate in this work, which every unbiased person aware of the big events of our time will have to acknowledge as necessary. Before criticizing and condemning spiritual science, people should ask seriously whether it wants to contribute sincerely to the progress of humanity. And when they have conscientiously informed themselves in this regard and have formed an opinion, then people will realize to what extent anthroposophical spiritual science has a right to participate in this task. For it wants sincerely and honestly to work toward the necessary progress, the necessary change in the thinking and outlook of humanity.

The Spirit and the Demonic in the Present and the Future

March 17, 1920

ONE OF THE most important assessments of the current chaotic world situation is undoubtedly that of the Englishman John Maynard Keynes. He presented his opinion in his book *The Economic Consequences of the Peace*.[1] His outer position in life qualified him to make such an assessment. During the war, he was assigned to the British Treasury and was able to establish the foundation of his later opinion out of the firsthand information he received there. In addition, he was one of the delegates working on the Treaty of Versailles. However, he resigned from this position as early as June 1919. Both his resignation and the conclusions he arrives at concerning the economic consequences of the treaty illuminate his view of the current world situation.

Initially, Keynes was one of those who considered Woodrow Wilson, the American who had been received with such great glory, to be a kind of prophet who would bring the world into order again.[2] Well, he changed his mind completely. Even when Woodrow Wilson was hailed by enormous crowds as liberator of the world, I have frankly and repeatedly expressed my opinion here in Switzerland—even in this city—that Wilson's empty and abstract talk and his manifestoes could not contribute anything to a true rebuilding of our devastated civilization. Thus, I am certainly justified now in pointing to the assessment of such a prominent person as Keynes. In his book, Keynes vividly and graphically characterizes Wilson's personality. He describes Wilson's arrival in Versailles, his participation in the negotiations, and his slowness in thinking that made him tag along behind everyone else. While the other delegates had already far advanced in their assessment of the situation, Wilson was still stuck on something that was discussed five, six, or even ten sentences earlier. He suffered from the slowness of his thinking. Keynes describes many other details concerning the personality of this supposed liberator of the world.

Keynes also wrote at length about the other political leaders involved in negotiating the peace treaty. He characterizes Clemenceau as a man who in a sense slept through and missed the whole development of Europe after the 1870s and whose goal in the peace negotiations was nothing else but to return the world to the conditions that prevailed in Europe in the 1870s.[3] In the same vivid way Keynes then describes Lloyd George as a man superior to all the others, a man with a certain instinct for sensing what the people around him were thinking, planning, and doing.[4]

We can see from all this that even Keynes, an astute observer, found it difficult to form a sound assessment because the events were so tremendous and powerful. One of the things that contributes to making the current world situation more and more chaotic is the inability of the leaders who have come into the spotlight of public life through the events of recent decades to cope with the great demands of our time. That is what we can learn from the above-mentioned book and its view of the situation. It also shows us that the destructive forces at work in the world today can by no means be properly assessed by those who have been called to political leadership. Keynes realized that this peace conference could not produce anything that would lead to a wholesome and beneficial development of European civilization, and therefore he resigned his position already at the beginning of the negotiations.

The way Keynes developed his assessment is very significant. In fact, all we need to do is to build something real on opinions that are based on the same foundations as Keynes's view. His assessment is based on calculation. Actually, nowadays we should listen only to people with a certain sense or instinct for coolly calculating the future based on forces still at work now. We have good reason to listen to them because most of the contemporary opinions are based on nationalistic and chauvinist or other prejudices. There are only a few people whose opinions are dictated by the objective facts, and Keynes is one of those few.

Keynes reflected on what would result, particularly for the economy, from the treaty the three above-mentioned leaders had concocted at Versailles. He looked at what would gradually have to happen in the European economy if the forces that were brought to bear at Versailles could work without any interference. And Keynes calculated—I want to repeat and underscore the word "calculated"—that nothing but the economic ruin of Europe would result from this peace treaty. Of course, the economic ruin will be accompanied by spiritual, cultural, and political disintegration.

Due to its contents, this book on the economic consequences of the Treaty of Versailles is quite interesting. But it becomes even more interesting because of its conclusion, for there Keynes openly admits to not having any idea about what to do or plan to get out of the chaos we find ourselves in. And with this admission he says something very important and summarizes it poignantly in one sentence. He says that we can only hope that something beneficial will result for European civilization from consolidating all available forces to develop a new condition of soul and new imaginations.

Ladies and gentlemen, this statement was made by a man who was intimately involved in these circumstances and who was called upon to participate in them. His exposition in this book proves him to be a man capable of cool calculation. A new condition of soul and a consolidation of all forces into a new perspective on the powers at work in our society—where can we find those? How can we achieve them?

Well, ladies and gentlemen, all we need is some objectivity and we will have to admit that the first step in that direction is to examine the fundamentals of contemporary public life without preconceived ideas. We have to look at the forces that are at work in our society. In earlier lectures I had the privilege to give here, I indicated the type of historical perspective that will allow us to understand the active forces in humanity. Above all, we have to examine certain symptoms that reveal what is active in the depths of human history.

To identify what is perhaps the most prominent of the forces involved in the work of destruction, I want to mention the basis of the contemporary world view as it has developed over the last three or four centuries. I do not mean to say that a world view constructed in some scholar's solitary study will then affect each individual soul and that our public affairs will then grow out of this world view. That is certainly not the case. However, our public affairs grow out of our willing and feeling, out of our emotional life and our thoughts, out of our total basic orientation. Similarly, our world view develops out of this total orientation, namely, out of our soul. Thus, we can study the symptom of world view to diagnose the condition of an era, its people, and their actions. The prevailing world view of today, except for the elements that have been handed down through tradition, has developed on the basis of the natural sciences, whose knowledge and insight are founded exclusively on studying the outer material world.

What does the world view of the natural sciences reveal upon closer examination? Perhaps only those able to admire this world view can evaluate it properly. I have certainly expressed my admiration for the natural sciences and their outlook with sufficient force and conviction in my previous lectures. And today's talk, too, is not motivated by opposition against the natural scientific outlook, which is certainly justified in its own sphere. After all, the natural sciences, particularly in their applications in technology and economy, have greatly advanced human civilization.

Nowadays, scientific knowledge has grown tremendously and its various branches have become highly specialized so that it can probably no longer be encompassed by any one individual. Nevertheless, let us assume someone were able to comprehend the whole vast realm of the natural sciences, from mathematics and mechanics to biology and the psychology derived from it. This admittedly hypothetical individual would undoubtedly gain many significant insights into various areas of nature. However, this person who is firmly grounded in the natural sciences and really comprehends their full scope will be the first one to admit that they cannot provide an answer to the essential question human beings have wrestled with since the beginning of time: What is the true nature of the human being and what is our relationship to the world. This question remains unanswered by the modern natural sciences.

Though the natural sciences have made an excellent beginning in developing theories about how our physical body has evolved from lower, animal-like forms, these same theories have led us far away from knowing what human beings really are in their relationship to the spiritual worlds. Not to acknowledge this openly will prevent us from understanding the inner impulses that impel people nowadays in their efforts to organize their public affairs or to destroy their public organizations. We may not always be conscious of our thoughts about our own nature and our relationship to the cosmos; nevertheless, these thoughts—even if they are unconscious and instinctive—influence our emotions and our decisions. Thus, these thoughts are the creators of our whole public, cultural-spiritual, political, and economic life. You need only look at things the right way to realize that our economic conditions are created by human beings, who in turn act out of the impulses in their soul. The economy is thus a reflection of what we think and feel about ourselves and our relationship to the cosmos.

The natural sciences have achieved much in understanding everything that is not human. Concerning the human being, however, they cannot answer our questions. Their strength is in providing information about the subhuman realms. But how does this information relate to the ideas and inner impulses we are to contribute to society, to our life together with other individuals and groups? Can the nonhuman realm give us an impetus for our actions and for our relationships with other people? That this is indeed not possible will become clear when we examine our relationship to language.

Basically, we are connected with each other through language. It is through language that we govern the economy and establish the political and spiritual-cultural conditions we live in. There is a very strange thing about language that is unfortunately usually not examined closely enough. To put the findings of the natural sciences into words, we always have to extend the meaning of words and phrases we use to talk about our inner life and our soul to nature. This is true even for the way we phrase the natural laws we admire so much as the great progress of modern humanity.

Sensitive people have always been aware of this, and Goethe was one of them. Goethe said people do not begin to grasp how anthropomorphic their outlook actually is. For example, when we describe a moving ball as "hitting" another and deduce from that observation the law of the conservation of momentum, we basically start out with the meaning the word "hit" has when we talk about our own organism. Careful study will show that every time we use language to express the findings of the natural sciences, relating only to the nonhuman realm, we have to use words and phrases originally referring to the human being.

How did our language acquire its meaning? There would be very little meaning if we could only imitate the mooing of cows and other animal sounds. So, how did language get its meaning? An objective study of human evolution reveals that all language content can be traced to the fact that in ancient times, in the far-distant past, people had a certain instinctive spiritual knowledge of nature that was accompanied by elemental emotions in their soul. Together with the will impulses and images expressed in myths, people also received spiritual insights and developed the content of their soul out of them. Later, in our time, this soul content filled the language of a time that is good at looking down contemptuously on what these instinctive spiritual capacities gave to people of an earlier epoch.

In our time of the flowering of the natural sciences, the words we use have not received any new meaning. It is historically extremely significant that in the last three or four centuries all languages of the civilized world have lost their old meaning. No new meaning could be poured into them because the natural sciences that achieved so much in our day are unable to provide such new meaning. And so, in our time, which we have to admire in many respects, we also see the languages of the civilized world being emptied of their ancient spiritual meaning.

As they lost their ancient instinctive meaning without receiving new meaning from the natural sciences, the languages of the civilized world degenerated to mere empty phrases, a development that has culminated in our time. These empty phrases lack any even limited meaning, and have in fact now achieved dominion over the world. And the four or five terrible years we have behind us revealed the peak of this dominion of the empty phrase; we are now virtually completely under its sway. And the only remedy is to give our language a new spiritual and conscious meaning. The old spiritual meaning, which people in ancient times acquired instinctively and which made language into a whole of words, not of empty phrases, is now gone. Present-day humanity can no longer believe in it. A new, conscious, spiritual meaning has to be attained.

Ladies and gentlemen, anthroposophical spiritual science, which is represented in the building in Dornach, consciously strives to complement the natural sciences and their great insights into nonhuman nature with conscious spiritual knowledge that is as lucid, logically consistent, and scientifically exact as those sciences. This spiritual knowledge then can tell us about our true nature and our relationship to the cosmos. However, before we can begin with such knowledge, we have to admit that while we will have to imitate the thoroughness of the methods of the natural sciences, these methods themselves cannot lead us to spiritual insights. To attain spiritual knowledge, we must apply above all those inner capacities we are to develop on the basis of anthroposophical spiritual science. In my book *Knowledge of the Higher Worlds and Its Attainment* as well as in the second part of my *Outline of Occult Science*, I have described how we can arrive at such knowledge through our own inner life.[5]

However, as I have repeatedly emphasized, to embark upon the path to this knowledge requires something we submit to only very grudgingly, namely, intellectual humility. But people nowadays are particularly proud of their intellectual development. Let me give you an example of what I mean by intellectual humility. When we give a volume of Goethe's poetry to a five-year-old, the child will most likely tear it up or play with it. She will certainly not get from the book what an adult reader does and what Goethe actually wrote it for. We have to gradually educate the child and develop her skills so that she can let Goethe's poetry work upon her in the right way. It is generally accepted that this kind of education and development of capacities is necessary; however, in their intellectual arrogance people do not want to admit that even after reaching adulthood and being equipped with the abilities to be acquired in ordinary life, they are still like a five-year-old trying to read Goethe's poetry when it comes to

95

understanding the world. Through self-discipline we first have to develop our soul capacities to be able to draw something from what is given to us in the world that can be compared to what the child will get from Goethe's poetry once she has reached adulthood, let's say, at age twenty-five.

To understand ourselves and to fulfill the Apollonian dictum "Know Thyself," we have to take the development of our soul capacities into our own hands. Tomorrow I will explain in more detail how this can be done. Today, I merely want to indicate in more general terms that it is indeed possible to strengthen our thinking through certain practices, which I will explain to you tomorrow. When our thinking has become strengthened to the point where it no longer merely follows passively our perceptions but is inwardly taken hold of by the will, it will become active and more intensive. Then we will know inwardly through direct experience that our thinking has developed into soul-spiritual perceiving.

Usually, our thinking is completely dependent on its instrument, the body and the nervous system. Once we have strengthened it, we can fully understand this dependence. We will realize that our thinking frees itself from the body as it becomes stronger through the exercises I have described in my books. Our thinking activity then is no longer guided and controlled by its bodily instrument. Our thinking will be strengthened and liberated from its instrument through certain meditations we can practice as objectively as we carry out an experiment in the lab or study the stars in an observatory. To use this enhanced thinking for a true perception of the world, we have to control our will through self-discipline. When this disciplined will combines with inner meditation and develops into will-permeated thinking—which is free of the body—then we will attain conscious spiritual knowledge.

In turn, this knowledge will then give us what people in ancient times received from their instinctive spiritual knowledge, meaning for our language. The old instinctive spiritual knowledge ceased—and, in a sense, human evolution was interrupted—and the natural sciences took its place so that we would feel impelled to fill our language with meaning out of our own being. We have to see from the signs of the times that we must acquire self-knowledge through conscious inner work, through developing our thinking into soul perception. That is the only way to fill our language once again with meaning and to eliminate the rule of the empty phrase.

Our spiritual knowledge will also help us realize that the outer world we perceive with our senses and in which we live between birth and death cannot lead us to anything spiritual. We ourselves bring spiritual content into the world when we descend from the spiritual worlds into the physical one at birth. As I said, we will talk about this in more detail tomorrow. We carry spiritual content into the world, and we develop it gradually, year after year, by means of our body. It is not the increasingly rich worldly content of our sensory experience that will make the spiritual realm become a reality for us; rather each of us as an individual carries the spirit into the world at birth.

Many people are afraid of what they as individuals have brought with them into the world at birth. They fear that it would lead them into all sorts of fantastic ideas if they were to use it. However, there are methods that help us avoid being led into fantasy. Once we realize that basically all spiritual content comes from the human individuality, we will readily admit that a wholesome development of this spiritual life is only possible when people have the opportunity to unfold their full potential. In other words, our spiritual development, the expression and revelation of our spirit, must not be dependent on any outside powers that are of use only here in the physical world.

The flourishing of the pure natural sciences and their insights into the nonhuman realm was accompanied by an increasing dependency of the spiritual-cultural life on the demands of society and economy rather than on what we bring into the world at birth. The same era that witnessed the growth of the natural sciences also saw the culmination of the omnipotence of the government; its tentacles are wrapped around all of spiritual-cultural life. For example, the government organizes the educational system, while the economy determines who can make his or her way into this sphere. At the same time, people have lost the ability to bring forth spiritual content out of themselves and to fill their language with spiritual meaning. As a result, in the scientific age, the spiritual-cultural life has become more and more dependent on the political and economic powers, a dependency that led to the worldwide dominion of the empty phrase.

This dominion of the empty phrase, of empty talk, is the front rank in the forces of the present-day organizations working toward destruction. Our language inevitably degenerates into empty phrases when we can no longer fill it with the spiritual substance we draw directly from our connection with the spiritual worlds. Just as inevitably, we will become so used to these empty phrases that we let ourselves be carried away by the mechanisms of our language. What bursts forth with primeval force out of our soul-spiritual core and is discharged into our language vanishes. This development is unfortunately only too

obvious these days. We live more and more intensively in
the mechanisms of language, a trend that has culminated
in recent years. In talking about the civilized world,
whether directly and personally or indirectly in print, people were actually talking about nothing. And while the
words were mechanically running along, the chaotic forces
that pushed us toward destruction developed.

I know very well that people are little inclined these
days to look at such subtle details of human life in connection with the causes of our present chaos. However, to
come up with clear concepts and opinions about these
causes, we must look closely at these minute details of our
soul life. There will be no harmony in our public affairs
until spiritual concentration and true spiritual science have
once again created in us the desire to fill our words with
spiritual meaning. New ideas and insights that first appear
in the sciences then push their way into other areas of life
and become predominant in society. A sense for observing
life will tell you that the characteristic way of developing
world views reveals its ultimate consequences in everyday
life. For a long time now, people have not wanted to know
about these connections.

At one time there lived here in Switzerland a blustering
fellow—I could call him a *poltergeist* to show you that I do
not overestimate him—by the name of Johannes Scherr.[6]
Through his blustering approach and opinions he spoiled
many of the sound ideas he presented to the public. In the
1860s and 1870s, he expressed a very significant opinion
on the basis of his thorough study of historical and social
conditions. He said that if the demon of materialism,
which is based entirely on what we see and experience in
the outer world, continues to hold sway, then it will also
gain entry into everything we do in our public affairs. It

will pervade our economy and the financial sphere. Eventually, a social structure will develop that will force us to admit, "Absurdity and nonsense, you have won."

Ladies and gentlemen, of course, nobody likes to listen to people like Scherr, and so his views were ignored. But now, fifty years later, in view of everything connected with the catastrophe of the world war, we have to admit that the prediction of Johannes Scherr that we will have to say, "Absurdity and nonsense, you have won," has come true. Scherr saw clearly how the spirit was squeezed out of human life, and in its place there appeared the demon of materialism. He developed an accurate prophecy from this observation.

People generally do not know that a world view or theory will eventually become the social and moral functioning of people two generations later; what was only a world view at first develops into actions later. People need to be much more aware of these connections. Our opinions and assessments of certain things should be much more thorough and realistic.

Not too long ago, a philosopher by the name of Richard Avenarius lived here.[7] He was a kindred spirit of Ernst Mach, and a pupil of the latter recently worked here in Zurich.[8] These philosophers have drawn the proper conclusions for their world view from the currently predominating demon of materialism—I call it a demon because mere knowledge of nature cannot fill our language with real meaning. The philosophy they developed and their way of life were plain and honest. You cannot tell by the looks of them that they are anything but good and upright citizens. But these days people should take note of something else; they should look at events and consider what the political philosophy of Lenin and Trotsky is.[9]

Well, what is the political philosophy of the Bolshevists? It is none other than that of Mach and Avenarius.[10]

The fact that some of these people have studied at the same time here in Zurich is not the only evidence for this. There is also an inner connection, namely, what is a world view in one generation develops into actions in the third generation. These actions reveal the causes at work in the world. However, these days, people want only abstract logical conclusions and do not understand that to deduce something logically does not make it a fact. But we have to look with true spiritual perception into the actual connections between things to see the seemingly most unlike things, such as the bourgeois world view of Avenarius— which grew out of the demon of materialism—resurrected in what will destroy all human society entirely and will lead all of European civilization into its grave.

This also implies that the dominion of the empty phrase is not limited to a particular area; it is a basic force permeating our whole society, especially our spiritual-cultural life. Things will not get better until our cultural-spiritual life is emancipated from what has become the basis of the empty phrase, namely, the sphere of politics and law and the economy. It must be built entirely on what the spirit brings forth out of itself, that is, on what each individual makes out of what he or she carries from the spiritual world into the physical one at birth. The only way to overcome the dominion of the empty phrase is to develop spiritual meaning.

There is another phenomenon closely allied with the empty phrase. Since in the empty phrase there is no connection between the words and their meaning, words can easily become carriers of lies. It is only a short step from the empty phrase to the lie. That is why lies have been so prevalent and triumphant in the last four or five years. Lies in turn contribute to the process of destruction we are headed for if we do not replace this demon with true spirit.

So, ladies and gentlemen, this is how things stand in one area of society, that of our spiritual-cultural life. Of course, there are still other areas, all of which are dependent in a certain sense on the spiritual-cultural life. If the empty phrase and talk without content predominate in our spiritual-cultural life, then what comes out of these phrases, especially what can be learned in social relationships, will also not be able to enter into our feelings and emotions. What develops in the feelings and emotions in our social relationships, and what is kindled in the interactions between individuals because we sympathize with each other, that is morality and will over time evolve into a habitual morality. Historically, laws can develop only out of this habitual and traditional morality.

However, laws will develop only when we keep the empty phrase out of the feelings that unfold in our relationships with each other. Instead, words filled with substance and thoughts must be integrated into these emotions. In this age of the empty phrase, our interrelationships cannot develop properly; only superficial relationships are possible. As a result, the predominance of the empty phrase in the sphere of the spiritual-cultural life of society is accompanied by the development of conventions in the area of social sensibility. There will be conventions, empty relationships, between people that can at most be regulated through contracts, instead of the direct and substance-filled relationship from individual to individual. In fact, even where whole nations are concerned, people are enthusiastic about contracts and treaties because they can no longer live out directly what can be revealed in the interaction between individuals. Convention has robbed another area of our society of its content: it has made our social relationships as barren as the empty phrase has made our soul life.

Of course, all this does not lead us beyond our physical being and to the laws born out of our inner being. For those laws can only come to life when words filled with thoughts flow from our head to our heart. True laws, which can thrive only in social relationships, belong to a true cultural-spiritual life filled with spiritual substance, as much as conventions belong to a cultural-spiritual life dominated by the empty phrase.

Thus, we have characterized two areas of our society; the third one, which is its basis, is that of our will. A conscious will that can integrate us into society so that we can contribute something to it out of our inner being can develop only when this will itself is impelled by true spiritual substance. The empty phrase cannot stimulate a truly conscious will in us. When our cultural-spiritual life becomes dependent on the outer political, legal, and economic conditions, it degenerates into empty phrases. And when our laws themselves are fed only by empty phrases, they become mere conventions. Similarly, if our will is not moved by the spirit, our economy and the area of human relationships will be based on mere routine rather than on the experience of life. Thus, we witness not only the emergence of the empty phrase and of conventions but also of routine in all areas of life and their outward expression, particularly in the economy.

Let me explain what I mean by characterizing our economy as dominated by routine. To look at our society and economy as they really are is to see that we must put an end to the currently prevailing chaos of everyone wanting to acquire things out of egoism without taking into consideration the relationship between our own individual production and that of society as a whole. Our economy has gradually slid into chaos, and it will recover only when the various professions and trades form associations so that the individual can see how he or she contributes to the whole through his or her production or consumption. In other words, people in different trades working in related industries and suppliers and consumers in a particular industry should form associations so that the resulting structure of the economy allows each person to see how his or her job fits into the circulation of goods and services. This is the only way for each individual to get a clear picture of his or her part in the economy as a whole. Then people will know not only how to do this or that job routinely, but also how what they are doing fits into the total context of the economy.

People will then do their work out of a different motivation; what they are doing will no longer be governed by superficial routine but by their practical experience of life and the idea they connect with it. This requires that people see themselves and their economic activity as part of the organism of humanity.

Because the empty phrase and conventions have taken hold everywhere, people have not been able to form such associations. Instead, they have been distracted from their real tasks and have become workers doing their work as a matter of routine. The routine has spread from the individual working mechanically in his or her job to the mechanism of our whole society and our financial system. The age of the empty phrase has become the age of routine. And that is what brought about the recent catastrophe, for which there may be this or that superficial reason, but whose deeper causes lie in the area I have just described.

When we examine objectively, without sympathy or antipathy, what prevails in our time, we have to admit that in the cultural-spiritual sphere it is the empty phrase, in the area of the law it is conventions, and in the economy it is routine. Only the forces I will describe in more detail tomorrow can lead us out of this situation. The empty phrase has to be replaced with words filled with substantial, experienced spirit; this can result only from an independent cultural-spiritual life that carries into the outer world what we bring with us at birth. This cultural-spiritual life will not be governed by something akin to natural laws, which are founded entirely on observation of the outer world. At the same time, conventions, which are determined externally, have to be replaced with living interrelationships that can develop when all citizens of age get involved in strictly democratic fashion in general human concerns. This is not something we bring with us at birth, but we develop it only in our relationships with our fellow citizens. Routine, which affects the transitory products of the economy, will develop into true practical life only if we arrive at a world view, based on a language filled with thoughts and free of empty phrases, that convinces us of the necessity to found associations.

We must found associations that will bear witness to the fact that what we produce in the economy is more than what can be accomplished by machines and forms a part of the total process of human evolution on earth. People will not arrive at such a view if they do their jobs only routinely, whether they work in factories, banks, or elsewhere. They will attain it only if they are linked to other people through associations and if they learn from others how their own production and consumption is connected to the social organization closest to them.

Through working together in associations people will establish something that goes beyond what we usually get from our economic activity. True, we have to be active in the economy, but our whole being transcends the economic realm, leaving behind the transitory and approaching the eternal. Ultimately, the economy teaches us that our practical activity here in this life is a lesson for us that we can carry with us over the threshold of death.

The spiritual contemplation of our time and the three above-described domains—that of the empty phrase, of convention, and of routine—leads to the realization that society must be organized in a threefold way. To become sound again, our cultural-spiritual life must become independent, our laws must be freed from convention and be based on the living, democratic interrelationships between adults, and our economy must be based on a true practical experience of life rather than on routine. However, these improvements will come about only if people connect with each other in associations. After all, it is only through such social connections that the economic activity of the individual can lead all of humanity to transcend itself and move from mere matter to the spirit. The dominion of the empty phrase means the rule of the demon in all areas of cultural-spiritual life. In the area of politics and law, conventions lead to the rule of the demon, and in the economy, routine leads to the same result. This demon must be replaced with spirit. This is possible and tomorrow I want to talk about how it can be achieved.

Our society will be cured of its current ills only if language filled with thoughts—that is, true spiritual life—will take the place of the empty phrase, if laws permeated by social sensibility replace conventions, and if a spiritualized economy takes the place of one based on routine—that is, an economy organized according to spiritual principles and based on associations. Indeed, our society will be destroyed if nothing is done to remedy its ills.

Nowadays we see all too many empty phrases, conventions, and routine as well as their result: chaos. For the future we need words filled with thought, spirit filled with substance, and living laws that have grown organically out of the working together of all adults. Then the spirit will have replaced the demon. In the economy, we need associations growing out of the spirit, and we need the elimination of routine through a true economy based on the spirit. That means that the demon of our time will have to be replaced with spirit in the future. We can rise above the pessimistic outlook seemingly justified by outer life and gain hope for the future by refusing to build on the hopes that might be thrown our way. Instead, we must build on our own will, which wants to achieve the victory of spirit over the demon out of its own power, persistence, and passion.

[A brief discussion followed.][11]

CONCLUSION

The first speaker mentioned an international language as a way to connect and integrate humanity. To talk about the advantages and disadvantages of this proposal would take us too far afield because it requires a really detailed and thorough discussion. Let us just assume that those striving for an international language have good reasons for doing so. You already know what has been attempted and accomplished in this direction.

Propagating this language through a kind of club, as has been done so far, is of course not sufficient. To have real practical significance, such a language would have to be presented to people in different ways than has been done so far. However, I do not want to speak out against an international language. You see, I know that everything we create artificially in our time will also have all the characteristic qualities of our era, namely, a certain rationality and intellectuality. I cannot help but admit that the intellectualism and the anti-elemental forces that have brought us so low also seem to be involved to a considerable extent in establishing this international language.

I can very well understand the views of those who wonder what will become of the originality of human self-expression in poetry and language in general when all of humanity accepts an abstract language. On the other hand, I have heard very beautiful poems in Esperanto, and I have certainly tried to gain an objective view of this issue.

Nevertheless, ladies and gentlemen, the issue of an international language does not touch on what I have been talking about today. For even in the hypothetical case that such a language would be introduced, it would still not contain anything else but empty phrases unless there is a renewal of substantial spirit. Whether we churn out empty phrases in Esperanto, English, German, French, or Russian does not make any difference. What matters is that we become able to bring substantial spirit into Russian, German, English, French, *and* Esperanto. That is what I have been talking about.

As I said, I do not want to object to the endeavors of those who want to introduce an international language. I think one aspect might be particularly fruitful to consider in this regard. It would be helpful if we succeeded in introducing an international language for our international economy. Perhaps it would then be possible to free up the other languages for the cultural-spiritual life as such, which, after all, always grows out of the individual. This will require that the other languages are allowed to develop individually without any interference from the thirst for conquest and dominance of the political powers.

Yet, I believe the hopes of those advocating Esperanto and similar things are built on even weaker foundations than the hopes of those who believe that a better age— though not a perfect one—will dawn if only a sufficiently large number of people works together on renewing our cultural-spiritual life out of the spirit. After all, people who truly understand reality cannot be among those who hope for a paradise on earth. Still, I think the latter group is more firmly grounded in reality than those hoping for the introduction of an international language.

The comments of the second speaker were essentially an interpretation of what I explained in my talk. I only want to add that in talking about such things, particularly on the basis on which I presented my lecture, we must not forget that we cannot simply approach people and make them better by instructing them. I have often used the following analogy for the pure method of instruction. I can tell a stove that it has the duty to warm the room, that its categorical imperative is to warm the room. I can preach at the stove all I want and present my arguments with all the reason and insight of Kant; yet that will not make the room any warmer. However, if I remain silent and simply put some wood in the stove and light it, then the room will get warm without any preaching.

It is the same with people. When we are concerned with the whole human being and not only with the part that can at most provide a theoretical echo for our efforts, then preaching is pretty much useless, for then we are dealing with people participating in a social entity. And the person as part of a social entity is different from the person as an individual. Before we can expect the individual to contribute somehow to the improvement of humanity through concentrating his or her thoughts, we must first make possible the fruitful development of such concentrated thinking. This development can occur only in a free cultural-spiritual life. You will find further details in my book *Towards Social Renewal.*[12] Thus, it is less a matter of examining what will be of use to the individual than of finding out what has to be done in the whole social organism so that the individual can truly unfold.

I published my book *The Philosophy of Freedom* for the first time in 1894.[13] Based on a spiritual world view, I presented a certain moral philosophy in that book that is particularly geared to the individual. This philosophy is based on the premise—and if we look at the problem of freedom seriously and realistically, we will have to accept this premise—that if it is possible to have intuitions on which to base the true freedom of the human being, then each individual must be able to contribute something we can build on in society. We must always keep our eyes on our interrelationships in society. Thus, in a certain sense, my book *Towards Social Renewal* is the supplement to my *Philosophy of Freedom*. In the latter, I examine the origin of the forces for freedom in the individual, and in *Towards Social Renewal,* I look at how we must structure the social organism to allow the free development of each individual. Basically, these are the two great questions we must deal with at present. A true answer to these questions will also shed some light into the chaos we are in.

I would like to add here that I have planned my talks for today and tomorrow in such a way that I presented today a critique of our time. I wanted to point out what exists in our time and how it has developed to its current state of drifting into chaos and of being equipped with tremendous forces of destruction. Tomorrow I would like to talk about what needs to be done to lead our nation, in the broadest sense of the term, and all of civilized humanity out of this chaos. I would like to show you how the forces that are already within us, especially in our social relationships, can be unleashed even though at present they are bound. Therefore, the positive perspective, which the last speaker apparently missed today, will be more obvious in tomorrow's talk. However, I had to explain what ails us so that we can develop out of this insight an understanding of the kind of will necessary for a wholesome development in the future.

I would like to conclude by saying that people who take the issues of the present seriously must not become followers of something traditional such as a "thousand-year Reich." They must not believe that we can establish a paradise here on earth, but they must be aware that every reality can unfold only the conditions of existence appropriate to it. In the life between birth and death we will arrive at a "yes" to this life only if we are able to offset the imperfections of this physical life with the prospect of a spiritual life. One of the greatest mistakes more and more people make in our time is to expect to receive everything that makes life worth living from the mere outer life. And that is why many social issues are formulated as questions about how we should arrange the outer life so that it can give people everything they might expect from paradise. People who are putting the questions like this will never find an answer. True and genuine answers can be found only if we are filled with a sense of reality. And tomorrow I will present the answer this sense of reality offers us to the great questions of our time.

Spiritual Forces in National Life and in Education

Zurich, March 18, 1920

YESTERDAY I EXPLAINED how the three destructive forces of the universal dominion of the empty phrase, of conventions, and of routine contribute to our current decline. As I indicated, the empty phrase has to be replaced with language filled with thoughts that are permeated by spiritual substance and that will affect our social relationships through language. We must eliminate conventions by renewing the cultural-spiritual life and replacing the former with what can develop only out of the living interchange between adults living in a democratic society. And for mere dull routine we have to substitute a spiritualized practical life. At first glance, these things seem to be merely superficial facts of modern life. In truth, however, they bring us face to face with what is rooted in our innermost core and at the same time is manifest in the most meaningful, serious, and decisive social conditions.

As I explained yesterday, to find one of the basic causes for the current state of our civilization, which is riddled

113

with destructive forces, we have to look at one particular symptom. What I am talking about is the fact I mentioned yesterday, namely, that for the last three or four centuries the natural sciences have been the basis of our world view, particularly of the world view that is to give rise to something new. Aside from that, there are only the traditional impulses for a world view. What is new and has stirred people for the last couple of centuries is the question of how a world view can develop out of the scientific foundations of human knowledge.

Small wonder, then, that under the necessity of having to construct a world view on this basis forces have developed in our soul that are particularly suited to create such a world view. A certain kind of thinking and willing has developed over the past few centuries and has reached its peak in our time. The natural sciences emphasize again and again that the goal of their exact and thorough methods is to explore the world of facts and not to let any personal interpretation or attitude enter into their findings. That mere natural science isolated from any human element will inevitably lead to one-sidedness was clear to many great minds, for example to Goethe.[1] He and others have pointed out in vain that true knowledge that can be used as the basis for a comprehensive world view must not be separated from the human being. They pointed out that even outer physical facts have to be looked at in connection with the human being.

On the other hand, we also have to admit that this science that excludes the human element has achieved great success in bringing the world of technology to its current level. All this technological progress would not have been possible without the influence of the kind of thinking that focuses exclusively on what nature offers to observation or on what can be proved in experiments. To understand the language of the facts themselves is the ideal this kind of thinking strives to attain.

The human will hardly enters into this kind of thinking, as those familiar with the exact and methodical approach of the natural sciences know. It is our will that motivates us as we carry out our tasks in life and interact with other people; in short, it influences us in everything we do as members of society. Still, the great triumphs of the natural sciences and technology could come about only because people have learned to keep their thinking as much as possible free from the influence of their will. This way of thinking has developed into a habit over the last three or four centuries.

While this kind of thinking can lead to great discoveries in the realms of minerals, plants, and even animals—but there only to a lesser extent—it does not give us any insight into the true nature of the human being. We have not developed any other ways of thinking besides this one, which is, so to speak, devoid of will, because in a sense we are afraid of everything that will enter into our thinking when we structure and organize it out of ourselves, through our will. In the process, fantasies of all kinds and arbitrariness can affect our thinking. People like to point out again and again that compared to the findings of the natural scientists, who focused only on what nature itself or their experiments revealed to them, the world views of certain philosophers who have allowed their will to influence their thinking seem fantastic.

However, people just do not know that we can permeate our thinking with our will in such a way that this disciplined and will-imbued thinking is as free of any arbitrariness as the thinking that restricts itself to outer facts and experiments. To develop a will-imbued thinking we have to carry out exercises in our soul with energy, care, and patience. As part of this process, people who want to be spiritual researchers and really want to penetrate into the spiritual world, the only source of true knowledge about ourselves, must repeatedly and methodically focus their soul on thoughts that will help them develop their will. They have to develop the same force of will in regard to these thoughts that we usually have only in regard to the outer world, where we love or hate and take up this or that activity while rejecting others. Concerning the outer world, we can only have opinions; at the same time, it also involves crises. What we learn in the outer world through our will and through the resistance we meet has to be carried into the world of our thoughts if we really want to explore the spiritual world. Then we will notice that our thoughts are gradually becoming will-permeated forces, imbued with their own inherent order and principles.

You have to keep in mind, however, that this process of inner work I have described somewhat abstractly takes a long time. It has to be carried out as methodically in the realm of the spirit as the experiments with precision instruments in chemistry or physics. Just as chemists and physicists carry out their experiments conscientiously and carefully, so spiritual researchers carefully weigh thoughts against each other and assess their effect on each other. In the process, they transform the abstract thinking, which has developed under the influence of the natural sciences over the last three or four centuries, into an inwardly living thinking, which is more a kind of spiritual perceiving of images than our usual abstract thinking.

This is one of the factors necessary to attain true knowledge of ourselves, for it is impossible to use abstract thinking to gain this knowledge, which has to be spiritual insight based on spiritual perception. Abstract thinking, which has its rightful place in the natural sciences, leads to absurd results when it is applied to our social conditions and community life. The more abstract our thinking, the more dogmatic and pigheaded we have become. Granted, the way of thinking that developed in the last three or four centuries makes us more critical, more conscientious, and more methodical. However, concerning our integration into humanity as a whole—or even into parts of it—we have become more and more dogmatic. Look at it carefully and you will see that when we adhere to the way of thinking that has made the natural sciences so successful, we get used to always being right. However, the other side believes itself to be right, too. If we take this way of thinking to the extreme, people basically will no longer have anything to say to each other.

Well, aren't these the conditions we are already living in now? People experienced in life who have gone through many ordeals and have wrestled for decades with the problems of human existence may feel compelled by the current stage of human development to talk about these problems in the commonly accessible concepts of spiritual science. However, nowadays they encounter everywhere very young people who have had no more than a decade and a half of life experience and yet insist on their own standpoint. They counter the rich experience of the older people with their own standpoint. Ultimately, in abstract terms, these greenhorns who can think just as logically as the experienced old people, are not all wrong, for the core of our present-day science is basically independent of human development. It is achieved more or less easily as soon as we have reached a certain degree of adulthood.

117

Thus, abstract thinking or intellectualism, which has developed to a high degree of perfection, gives us something we want to share with others; however, the others already learned the same thing by themselves. Human beings need to communicate. However, no communication is possible when other people are not inclined to receive what we can tell them but only counter it with their own standpoint.

The way of thinking that has made the natural sciences so successful cannot be applied to our social conditions and community life because it will lead us to want to share something that others do not want to receive because they believe they know it already. When we think carefully about the basic orientation of our present-day soul life, we will realize that many of the destructive forces at work in our society, pushing people apart rather than bringing them together, are the result of the above-described peculiarities and social consequences of abstract thinking, which is so eminently suitable for the natural sciences.

Spiritual science will lead us beyond this way of thinking because it cultivates our will, of which we remain unaware in our conventional way of thinking. Spiritual science pushes this will into our thinking and thus develops in us a will-imbued thinking, the only kind of thinking that can enable us to achieve true knowledge of ourselves. However, this is only one side of the issue. In addition, influenced by the way of thinking developed through the natural sciences, people have added will devoid of thoughts to this thinking that lacks the will element. This is the duality making up the modern human being; on the one hand there is the thinking that lacks will and on the other the will devoid of thoughts.

118

Spiritual science tries to push the will into our thinking, and at the same time it also trains spiritual researchers to be as objective about the results of their own willing—that is, their actions—as they usually are only in regard to outer events. To embark upon the path of spiritual research requires faithful observation of our own actions and our own will. In a sense, we have to rise above ourselves and accompany ourselves through life on a higher level, so to speak. This higher self must observe us in the same way we usually study phenomena of nature or experiments. Only then will we learn to develop thoughts about something that for the last three or four centuries has largely been governed and motivated by our most personal emotions. This is true particularly in the case of people in certain radical and extremist circles. Through the process described above, we will become able to understand in our thoughts what is usually completely ignored and remains in the unconscious.

And because we are made up of the two above-mentioned elements, abstract scientific knowledge about nature, which is limited to the nonhuman realm, is completely separated from our social impulses, which now work only as personal instincts. The natural sciences have advanced to certain heights and their way of thinking has led to a certain kind of education. And in Eastern Europe— and unfortunately this trend will not remain confined to the East—people are nowadays trying to develop principles for the organization of community life and society on the basis of that education. However, as we can clearly see in the East, social policy based on the natural sciences cannot do more than organize the most chaotic human instincts; it does so in such a way that this organization will inevitably push humanity toward its ruin.

All these things are connected to what has gained pre-dominance in recent centuries, and we have to see everything in context. We have to cultivate the element of will in our thinking and then, as I have indicated, the thinking in our willing; you'll find the exact description of this process in my book *Knowledge of the Higher Worlds and Its Attainment* and also in the second part of my *Outline of Occult Science.*[2] Only when we establish a spiritual science on this basis, a science able to understand the true human essence, will such a science not be powerless when faced with the whole human individuality. At present, conventional science is at a loss when faced with the totality of the human personality because thinking that does not receive any impulses from the will is merely an activity of the head; it is intellectualism and does not impart any strength for living.

The spiritual knowledge that gradually develops into a world view on the basis I have outlined here, will affect not only our thinking and our intellect, but also our whole being. Because this spiritual knowledge grows out of our will, out of will-imbued thinking, it can fruitfully integrate this thinking into society and community life. By carrying thoughts into the will, spiritual knowledge stimulates us to a thinking that leads to a genuine practical experience of life rather than to mere routine. Truly practical life must be based on ideas, on spirit-imbued will.

We need this world view based on spiritual science above all in the area of the cultural-spiritual life that is the most important for the general public, that is, in education, in the school system. The inner truth of the principles of spiritual science I just described can be tested particularly in the field of education. In the Waldorf school I already mentioned, which was built in Stuttgart under the aegis of our friend Emil Molt, the teaching methods are based on spiritual science.[3] Yet, this school was not founded for the purpose of propagating our philosophy. People are not telling the truth when they claim that this school wants to instill anthroposophical spiritual science into children instead of the traditional world views. That is not the purpose of a Waldorf school; it was established so that the spiritual science we are talking about here can affect people's will and permeate their actions. The point is that what remains mere idea and theory in other philosophies leads to a methodological approach in spiritual science. Thus, what matters is not so much *what* the children in the Stuttgart Waldorf school are taught as *how* they are taught. In the Waldorf school our spiritual science becomes the foundation for the methods, the activities, and intentions of the teachers.

Obviously, our teaching methods have to be based on a true knowledge of the human being. This true knowledge, however, can be achieved only with the methods I have outlined here today. They teach us to distinguish in our inner soul-spiritual being different developmental phases in the human being. These phases often receive only cursory attention even from scientists who think themselves so conscientious and thorough. There are certain obvious changes in children at the time of their second dentition around the age of seven. A closer look reveals that this is not all; the children's entire soul life also undergoes a metamorphosis at that time. In the first seven years, children's behavior, inclinations, and capacities are determined to a large extent by the principle of imitation. They empathize with what goes on around them and imitate it. However, the second dentition marks the beginning of the phase when children are more disposed to respond to authority.

In other words, up to about the age of seven, children naturally and innately imitate the adults around them even in their gestures and their way of speaking. The children will live themselves into the imponderables, into the thoughts and ideas streaming from their environment toward them. However, by the time they reach the age of seven, children need a person to look up to. They need to feel that this person knows the right thing to do; they need an authority figure. Though people rail against authority nowadays, we have to keep in mind that between the ages of seven and the beginning of puberty children need to be guided and influenced by an authority figure if they are to develop in a healthy way.

This is the second developmental phase, which occurs between the second dentition and the beginning of puberty at the age of approximately fourteen. I use the word "approximately" because this is not a matter of juggling figures; what matters is the important phases, the transformations and metamorphoses over the course of our life. Then, around the age of fourteen, human beings begin to mature sexually, and a complete transformation of soul takes place. As a result, the young people become able to develop their own opinions and to confront the world with their independent inner judgment of it. They have outgrown the previous phase, between the ages of seven and fourteen, when they need an authority figure to look up to.

Now, the phase between the second dentition and the onset of puberty is when children are taught in school; these are their elementary school years. There are also other stages, sub-phases, so to speak, we can distinguish in this second phase between the ages of seven and fourteen. The drive to imitate, which governs the children's first seven years in their innermost being, weakens after age seven; yet it is still there and is evident more or less strongly into their ninth year. Through spiritual science we can develop a lively sense for this interplay between the children's capacity to imitate and their need for an authority figure to look up to, and then we will see each child as a unique challenge to our teaching abilities, regardless of how large the classes are.

Once teachers and educators have taken up spiritual science, they will no longer adhere to an approach based on standards and abstract principles derived from intellectualism, telling them how they must teach. No, teachers who have undergone training in spiritual science see each child as new and unique, just as an artist views each of his or her creations as new and unrepeatable. In spiritual science, there are no abstract didactic principles; instead, the teachers empathize with the child, and their approach is based on the child's inner being. They work on solving the riddle of the soul-spiritual that is concealed in the child and only manifests itself in his or her physical body.

Spiritual perception and knowledge lead us back to our inner core of unmediated aliveness, and this is what must be applied in education. That is not the case with intellectualism and abstract knowledge. If I understand something in the abstract—well, then I have "got" it and can carry it with me through life. At most, I will remember what I have learned. In spiritual knowledge and perception, however, things are very different. After only a few steps toward this knowledge, you will realize that it does not lead to anything you can merely remember. In that respect the insights of spiritual science are like the food we have eaten today; it will not nourish us if we merely remember it tomorrow and on the following days. We are not satisfied with just remembering what we ate four weeks ago. But we are satisfied when we remember some abstract concept we understood and learned four weeks ago. Spiritual knowledge and perception, on the other hand, becomes interwoven with our inner being; it takes root in our being, is assimilated, and has to be reenlivened again and again. In the process, it becomes part of the phenomena of our life.

Spiritual researchers who, at the age of forty, stop cultivating a continuous lively relationship to the knowledge to be gained will starve for a lack of soul- spiritual content, just as we would starve if we stopped eating at the age of forty. Abstract knowledge, which has gained so much ground because of the natural sciences, is content with mere phenomena; it leads to once-and-for-all, final conclusions. Spiritual knowledge, on the other hand, brings us into a living relationship to our surroundings; it must continuously be renewed if it is not to wither and die. Spiritual knowledge functions on a higher level of our life as food does on a lower one.

What I just said should convince people that spiritual knowledge is radically different from the kind generally believed to be the only one possible. Just think of the effect we will have when this spiritual knowledge imbues the teachers, permeating their thoughts, intentions, and actions just as iron permeates and enlivens our blood. Imagine the results when teachers' outlook is based on spiritual knowledge and on the conviction that each individual has to be approached in a unique way—the knowledge that methods that worked before cannot simply be applied again and that each child has to be seen as a new riddle for the teacher to solve. Clearly, only this outlook will lead to a true and living approach to teaching.

There is a lot of talk these days about educating the individual, and all sorts of wonderful abstract principles have been developed for that—but nothing will be achieved in this way. The only way to accomplish anything in our time, which demands life and not abstractness, is to establish education as an art. This art of education studies the inner being of each child anew and forgets about theories of knowledge just as artists forget about aesthetics and throw everything overboard in order to create something. After all, what good are principles and theories about the beautiful in shaping the clay? Those who know what it means to create artistically will agree with me. Principles and rules for teaching are of little use when we are to decipher the riddle of the soul-spiritual in the child and help it unfold. This task requires that we as educators become artists, and this will be possible when spiritual science becomes a living part of our civilization.

As a result, we will realize that between the age of seven and nine, when the children's urge to imitate and their need for an authority figure balance each other, we have to develop their will rather than overemphasizing their intellect. During this time, we must teach subject matter that is based on conventions in an artistic way, and content that speaks mostly to the children's intellect must not be introduced as based only on convention. This includes the shapes of the letters in the alphabet as well as writing and reading in general, all of which are based on convention though they are derived from an ancient pictorial form of writing. In the Waldorf school, we teach writing and reading—at first, writing—in an artistic way. The children at first draw and paint the forms out of which they can then develop the letters. In other words, they start with the artistic and then proceed to the intellectual. To allow the

125

inherent needs of the child to unfold properly in this developmental phase, all teaching must be based on this artistic approach.

Now, after the first few months of classes in our Waldorf school, we can see that it is possible to really work out of this artistic element. In music, singing, and eurythmy— which for the children is nothing else but ensouled sound—we can give the children something their inner nature calls for and requires. All this makes their artistic sense flexible and inclines the children to see the whole world in an artistic way. Then at the age of nine, when the children begin to establish a boundary between them- selves and the outside world, we can teach them gradually to observe nature and to describe it; in other words, we can develop science out of art.

However, we always have to keep in mind that we are dealing here with human beings. I know this may sound trivial, but it has to be said, for the schedules our children get in schools nowadays ignore this fact. There is nothing more contrary to sound educational methods than the cur- rent practice of teaching children something different every forty-five minutes. For example, forty-five minutes of religious education, followed by a forty-five-minute les- son in arithmetic or writing, and so on. In the Waldorf school we base our methods on the laws manifest in the soul- spiritual being of the children. Accordingly, we teach one subject exclusively, for example, arithmetic, for three, four, five, or even six weeks without a specific schedule. When we have worked through a certain part of the curric- ulum in that field, we go on to another subject. Thus, our teaching becomes concentrated, and at the end of the school year we can summarize and review all the material we have covered. In contrast, the schedule as we have it now actually prevents us from practicing the true art of education.

The approach I described will lead to real achievements in the education and guidance of children and the curriculum requirements are based on the developmental needs of the children. When I gave the course preparing the Waldorf teachers for their task, I strove above all to develop a curriculum based entirely on what children need at age six, seven, eight, and nine, and from there on until the age of twelve or fourteen when they enter puberty. Through spiritual science we gain an understanding of the human being, and we can tell from the innate, natural development of the individual what we need to do from year to year. We know what we need to do when we read the faces of the children sitting before us in the classroom with profound pedagogical understanding. This is how spiritual science can bring life directly into one of the most important areas of society, namely, education. Of course, I cannot go into much detail here but only give you an outline of the essential points.

Abstractions and the great achievements of technology are of no help to us when human beings are to be brought together. The true art of education springs only from spiritual science. It requires that the cultural-spiritual sphere be liberated from the interference of politics and the economy through the threefold ordering of the social organism. Actually, it is only because there is a loophole in the Education Act of the state of Württemberg that we were able to establish the Waldorf school and operate it as a free school where we can really work on the basis of our educational and artistic principles. It is not necessary to become a spiritual scientist to accept spiritual science. We can accept the findings of modern chemistry or astronomy without becoming a chemist or an astronomer; all we need is sound common sense. Similarly, we only need common sense and an open mind to take in what the spiritual researcher brings to light out of the depths of the soul. To be imbued with the knowledge we gain out of will-filled thoughts and thought-filled willing can give us the necessary zest for life that modern humanity lacks because it is asleep to these things. We need this zest for life if things are to get any better.

What is needed to rebuild our civilization will not magically appear out of nowhere. No, a sufficiently large number of people has to demand forcefully what is necessary. Modern humanity is able and predisposed to demand the great goals in life out of its conscious will. We have spent enough time pursuing a policy of looking diplomatically at ... [gap in the shorthand record] and then saying that things will get better somehow. Nowadays people realize that things are getting worse with every passing day; yet each day they believe again that the new status quo will last. People have no sense at all for discovering the force of the upswing in the midst of our decline. As in education, so also in our society as a whole, we need to look for the forces that can lead to a rebuilding ourselves. And here, too, these forces can only come from the spirit, from knowledge and perception of the spirit.

Think of the two soul elements I described and their relationship in our society. On the one hand, there is the abstract thinking everyone has, regardless of whether the individual has grown up in a shoemaker's workshop and is the child of a shoemaker or ... [gap in the shorthand record]. On the basis of this thinking, which is independent of personal considerations, we develop our standpoint. Of course, we do not really need all of these standpoints, for every individual is entitled to have his or her own and could just as well and happily live alone with it. We do not need to live in a community with other people if we each have our own standpoint and nobody has the right to tell the others anything.

Spiritual science leaves behind all standpoints and this insistence on one's own. Instead, it makes people more receptive to life and to a true schooling. Once you are familiar with anthroposophical spiritual science as it is represented in our building in Dornach, each person you meet in life will become an interesting challenge for you. Especially in education it is important that each child is an interesting challenge for the teacher. In our physical life, we feel hungry for outer nature and desire to connect with it. Similarly, spiritual researchers feel a need to consider again and again what other people mean, what they think, feel, and want. To the greatest extent possible, spiritual science connects us with other people.

Above all, spiritual researchers do not react to other world views they might read about the way most people do. Students of spiritual science do not so much ask whether something is true or false, for that question is usually decided on the basis of one's own standpoint, and I have just explained what I think about standpoints. No matter how great an error this or that person presents in words or deeds, once we are imbued with spiritual science, we will be able to see what others reveal in their life as a complement and addition to our own being. Just as natural scientists want to observe their experiments, so spiritual scientists feel the need to look closely at everything human. If they develop a world view, it will become a social impulse, because it does not separate people but connects them. This world view of spiritual science once again brings individual life into what otherwise remains merely an abstract standpoint anyone can have.

Spiritual scientists receive revelations from everything human, including infants who can merely babble or simply just look at the world with their baby eyes. That is why the findings of spiritual science, once they are accepted, will become an impulse for our social relationships. The natural sciences emptied human language of its thought content and created the empty phrase instead. Spiritual science will once again enclose living, spiritual substance in our language. By connecting people again as individuals, spiritual science will make our language the most important means for social improvement in the near future.

As I said, our will has become dependent on mere emotions and purely personal instincts precisely because our knowledge has become increasingly abstract. Because spiritual science derives its content out of thought-imbued will, it serves as a basis for more far-reaching interests than we can develop out of merely personal feelings or egoism. The latter, egoism, ultimately has become the determining influence in society in the last three or four centuries. If we cannot ascend through knowledge ... [gap in the shorthand record] to the human level, if we cannot feel imbued with everything human, then we have nothing to contribute to society but egoism.

However, once the cultural-spiritual realm is autonomous, and we have established an independent art of education—as I have briefly described it today—once we can imbue our will with ideas, we will be able to build a bridge between individuals in our economy. We will be able to form associations in the various trades and professions as well as associations of consumers and manufacturers; the structure of our economy will be based on what

130

one person can learn from another. Routine will then be transformed into practical life.

The more closely we look at human life, the more we will be convinced of the necessity of a threefold structure of the social organism. As a result, the economy will be stimulated by a will imbued with ideas, and the cultural-spiritual life ... [gap in the shorthand record]. At the same time, what happens in the relationships between individuals—nowadays they are governed by convention to such an extent that people want convention even between different countries, for example, the League of Nations—will become a living element in a nation's system of laws. The latter will be an equal partner of the independent cultural-spiritual life and the autonomous economy in the threefold social organism.

The example of education shows how spiritual science will affect our nation and society. You can see that spiritual science must be the foundation on which the threefold social organism has to be built.

Just look at all the things that have come about under the influence of the two elements of soul I have described! There is the abstract thinking that transcends all human individuality; it is the same in all people who have acquired the skill of logical, abstract, and intellectualistic thinking. And because this thinking is the same for all people, what we cannot learn abstractly but have to acquire in our relationships with others is necessarily based on the subhuman element, on our egotistical instincts. Thus, in the age of Darwinism, people observed the struggle for existence among animals—even there this concept has only limited validity—and natural scientists wanted to become social scientists and politicians and set up the struggle for existence as the norm for human life, too.

Indeed, it is true that the struggle for existence would also rage in human life if our egotistic instincts alone were to affect society.

This struggle for existence is precisely what Lenin and Trotsky want to establish; they will only organize people's egoism.[4] This is obvious to everyone who understands contemporary life. Everything else will only mask this essential fact. We can already see the essential, inner lie of Leninism, which promises people mountains of gold and shorter working hours, and so far has only introduced a twelve-hour working day because the mechanism it intends to establish requires longer working hours.

Nevertheless, our abstract thinking, which is the same in everybody, will never agree to this struggle for existence, but will always reject it. It will always be dissatisfied with this principle and will continue to strive for harmony and for an end to the struggle for existence. However, if we do not pour true spirituality into this abstract intellectualism, it will be too weak to drive the egoism out of our social relationships and our society. By the same token, egoism will remain brutal if we do not inject it with the insights into the human being that only spiritual knowledge and perception can provide. This dualism of abstract intellectualism on the one hand and the reign of the instincts on the other can be balanced out only when both elements are imbued with spirit.

Once thoughts are spiritualized, they will be accessible to each individual and make us into people who do not always have to be right—people who can only give to others what the latter do not want—but who are continuously interacting with others, communicating with them not in the language of empty phrases but in that of thoughts. This language can develop only in a cultural-spiritual life that is not based on mere memory, but, like hunger and thirst, requires daily renewal and metamorphosis—in short, a cultural-spiritual life that must renew itself continuously even if it has already advanced to its highest level. All this requires that our instincts are permeated by the kind of thoughts that originate in the way I described. People will then be able to work in their associations for goals that transcend the individual; then our economy will be spiritualized.

Indeed, we see the necessity of the threefold ordering of the social organism everywhere in modern life. The threefold social order is not a utopian concept. Only people who have no sense of reality and are utopians themselves will call the threefold social order utopian; they have to cast aspersions on anything that does not fit into their utopian ideas.

However, the concept of the threefold ordering of the social organism is taken out of life in its fullness, which calls for permeation with what we can learn through spiritual perception. As human beings, we need this spiritual perception. To solve the pressing social problems of our time we must realize that human beings are not merely beings of nature.

Years ago, when theoretical materialism had its heyday, people who could see that it would lead to practical materialism got worked up about it and opposed it. Yet, we cannot help noticing that the people who became theoretical materialists, such as Haeckel and others, were bright people.[5] We are confronted here with the remarkable fact that truly bright people became materialists. How could this be? As will be particularly obvious to spiritual researchers, these people became materialists because the abstract way of thinking that developed over the last three or four centuries can only be explained on the basis of materialism. The way of thinking that has brought the natural sciences to their predominant position needs the tools of the brain and the physical body. This kind of thinking ceases when we die.

However, when we pour will into our thoughts and are not guided by observation of nature and experiments alone, when we imbue our thinking with what arises out of the will, then we arrive at a kind of thinking that is free of the body and is truly soul-spiritual. Materialism was right for the way of thinking that has gained prevalence over the last three or four centuries and has reached its peak in our time. This way of thinking can be explained only in terms of materialism. That is why some of the brightest people of the second half of the nineteenth century became materialists. The only question they had to deal with was that of the nature of the ordinary way of thinking that has reached such heights in the natural sciences. This question can be answered only on the basis of materialism. In its own way, materialism is indeed right. People who do not realize that materialism is valid and right in its own limited field cannot be spiritualists in the sense of anthroposophical spiritual science. To think one has to choose either materialism or spiritualism is to be on the wrong track. For materialism is indeed valid and legitimate in its own sphere. We must be aware that to save and preserve the soul-spiritual realm, we have to go beyond the way of thinking we are so proud of nowadays.

Clearly, then, no desirable social structure will ever develop if we continue to base our social order only on our usual egotistic emotions. These emotions can be the basis of the struggle for existence, but not of the realization of Lenin's social dream. A true social order can be established only when we pour the soul-spiritual—as I have described it today and as it emerges from the world view that is based on spirit perception—into our social conditions and our community life.

Then people will understand, and life will verify for them, what Goethe envisioned when he contemplated our true relationship to nature. Goethe realized that once we learn about the wonderful stars above us and about the various realms of nature all around us, we have to look at ourselves as we relate to nature, assimilating it, transforming it, and letting it rise again within us in a new, higher, soul- spiritual form that continues to work on us. Goethe put this very nicely when he said:

Since man represents the pinnacle of nature, he sees himself as a complete being who in turn has to produce a pinnacle. To that end, he strives upward, imbuing himself with all perfection and virtues, and calls to his aid his ability to select, to create order and harmony, to lend significance. Finally he reaches the level where he can produce art, which will now occupy a preeminent place next to his other deeds and works.[6]

This thought, which can be found in Goethe's book on Winckelmann, is complemented by another one, also from that book.

When man's nature functions soundly as a whole, when he feels that the world of which he is part is a huge, beautiful, admirable, and worthy whole, when this harmony gives him pure and uninhibited delight, then the universe, if it were capable of emotion, would rejoice at having reached its goal and admire the crowning glory of its own evolution. For, what

135

purpose would those countless suns and planets and moons serve, those stars and milky ways, comets and nebulae, those created and evolving worlds, if a happy human being did not ultimately emerge to enjoy existence?[7]

Only this attitude, which leads us through nature and beyond it and to our higher self, to the soul-spiritual in us, can be the basis for a rebuilding of our social order. To establish this foundation we must be willing to look at the insights we receive from researching our cultural-spiritual life as such.

Consequently, changing and transforming the outer social institutions will not lead to the improvements we have talked about. No matter how much we change the existing institutions, they will not be the basis for a rebuilding. Renewal will be possible only if we face the destructive forces within ourselves. For all the externals confronting us in our life actually originate in our innermost being. To make progress, we must change our ways, change our way of thinking. That is why things will not get better until a sufficiently large number of people gets up the courage to embark upon this process of change. Ultimately, constructive forces must emerge from our courage to ascend to the spirit, so that—as I said yesterday at the end of my talk—this spirit can gradually but surely eliminate the demonic forces.

[A discussion of the lecture followed]

CONCLUDING COMMENTS

Ladies and gentlemen! Mr. B.'s remarks give me no reason to add much in my concluding comments. He presented an example of how the contributions of our spirit-filled thinking are judged by the abstract modern way of thinking. That is why I would like to say a few words about the Waldorf curriculum to clear up any misunderstandings.

I said the Waldorf school curriculum aims at concentration. I did not say, however, that there should not be any variety. Of course, we could argue about whether we should create variety by replacing, for example, arithmetic with another subject after three or perhaps after five weeks or whether something else might be better. This is purely a question of didactics and cannot be resolved through arguing about it but only on the basis of facts. However, aside from that, the curriculum aims at concentration so that a certain amount of material can be covered without the obstacle and the interruptions of the conventional schedule. For three to six weeks, or for as long as is necessary, we cover a certain amount of material in a subject without being interrupted by anything else. Of course, in our teaching we take the being of the child into account.

To prevent misunderstandings, I would like to describe for you what happens in a classroom of the Waldorf school, for example, in the fifth grade of grade school—of course, I could just as well have taken the first grade as my example. Anyway, lessons start a few minutes after eight in the morning. In the first two hours, we concentrate on a subject that is scattered in the conventional schedule over several shorter periods of time. In other words, in the first two hours of the day, until about a few minutes after ten, we work in a concentrated way on the usual school subjects. During this block of time, the children will study, for example, arithmetic for a few weeks, then grammar for several weeks, and so on.

After these two hours, there follows what enhances concentration through the way it is presented, namely, foreign language instruction. In Waldorf schools we teach English and French even to the youngest children. It is very impressive to see the little ones come into their foreign language class and to see the great pleasure they have in the great progress they have made after just a few weeks of classes. In these language lessons, the children are taught to use the foreign language. Thus, for about five or six weeks the first graders learn French until about eleven o'clock and English until noon. Then they go home for lunch.

A few afternoons a week—of course, there are enough free afternoons; that is part of the variety we want—they return for lessons in singing, music, and eurythmy, ensouled gymnastics, and ensouled art of movement. This ensouled art of movement consists not only of physiological gymnastics—which is taught too, of course—but also of movement filled with spirit. In a sense, with eurythmy the children are given a kind of mute language, and they find their way into it extremely well. When there are eurythmy presentations on special festival days, the children are eager to participate and show a very lively enthusiasm. Thus, there is absolutely nothing to the claim that our curriculum lacks variety and that we do not take into account what is appropriate to the nature of the children.

Of course, some people will object that we change the subject areas whenever the children get bored—well, ladies and gentlemen, it is the task of the educators to make sure that the children are never bored. In the Waldorf school the children may be naughty once in a while; they may be getting too big for their breeches, but we take care that they do not want the lessons to end just because they are bored. In the short period since our school opened, I have paid it two longer visits, and each time I was in charge of teaching. Thus, I could see for myself that our methods do indeed bring life into the classroom.

Ladies and gentlemen, if we want to get beyond talking about equal rights for all and want actually to establish them, we should not go on and on about the difference between employer and workers. In spite of all the talk, this difference still exists; that is simply a fact. And all the talking will not wipe out this difference. In the Waldorf school, however, the worker's child sits next to that of the employer. The children are all taught together, and that is how we can establish equal rights for all in a concrete way. All the talk and agitating about how there should not be "employers" and "workers" will not get us anywhere. Rather, we must provide justice and equal rights for everybody.

In short, mere talking is not going to resolve the issue; only creating and achieving goals and working for a true solution to our social problems will do that. Adding more and more propaganda phrases when we really need to take action will keep us from making even the first step toward improvement. What is important these days is to know the difference between mere talk and action. If we cannot distinguish between the talker and those who want to do something, we will never get ahead. Instead, the talkers will talk our social order to death. Pretty talk does not get us anywhere nowadays, not even when it is about equal rights for all. Equal rights have to be established, merely talking about them will accomplish nothing.

Let me ask you another question. Shouldn't the material preconditions be provided for economically disadvantaged people to allow them also the opportunity to take part in the cultural-spiritual realm? I contributed an article entitled "Ideas and Bread" to one of the latest issues of the *Journal for Threefolding of the Social Organism* to counter the common prejudice that all we need to do to solve our social problems is to provide work and a living for all.[8] Particularly those who are satiated and able to feed themselves well again today are wont to point this out. That is easily said, but the important thing is that people see a purpose and meaning in their work. On the other hand, nothing is achieved when others claim that what we need to do is provide bread for all people so they will advance spiritually and culturally or at least can be taught to advance. After all, spiritual work is necessary before we can earn our bread. We have to organize things and integrate the work being done into some kind of a social structure; only then can we earn our bread.

Central Europe is now being engulfed by a terrible famine—even though times were not so good before either, but we won't talk about that now—not because the bread suddenly eludes us, but because the catastrophe of the war has pushed us into a social order where no bread is earned, an order where no ideas are at work that could enable people to earn their bread. The ideas that were worshipped by our leaders up to 1914 have been reduced to absurdity through the events of the last five or six years; they are dead. We need new ideas—to rebuild our social order and to enable us to earn our bread. If we cannot open our minds to new ideas, we will not see a healthy future development.

It is strange how clearly we can see in individual instances that people do not want to face the truth. One of the most radical people, certainly up to 1914, was Duke Kropotkin.[9] After he had returned to Russia, we could hear that if only Russia could get bread from the West, then things would get better there. At the same time, Kropotkin was said to be writing his book *Ethics*. You see, this is what has brought us to ruin: on the one hand, people have a material life, and on the other, they have an abstract cultural-spiritual life that does not affect the former at all.

Spirit is manifest not when we worship it, but when it becomes able to master and organize matter. It is too bad that religious denominations nowadays only want to provide people with a beautiful content for their leisure hours. At most, we find the phrase "God bless us" on the first white page of the ledger, even though what is entered there as debits and credits does not always justify having this phrase in the front of the book.

One of the symptoms of the decline in our time is that we have lost the ability to find the bridge from what we profess spiritually to our material and practical life. Instead, the prevailing attitude is that the material life must be completely separate from the spirit. After all, spirit is something very noble and sacred, and therefore it has to be kept free of matter. No, the spirit is not to be kept separate from matter so that people have access to it only after they leave the factory or on Sunday afternoons. The spirit is to be carried into the factory and to organize the machines and the workers in a spiritual way. It is the task of the spirit to permeate material life. And we will perish if this does not happen, because our cultural-spiritual life is so abstract and our unspiritual material life is governed by routine. For things to get better, the spirit must become so powerful that it can master matter.

Spiritual science does not want to lead people to an unworldly spirit foreign to matter, but to the spirit that can rule human life. We find this spirit not only when we are glad to finally be able to leave the factory, but we can also gladly carry it into the factories so that every one of our movements is done in light of this cultural-spiritual life.

To strive for the spirit we are talking about here is not seeking an unpractical spirit. The spirit we are striving for does not just contribute empty and nice phrases we can enjoy in our leisure hours, but it rules matter; it can organize and be closely connected with our everyday life. Whether we will stumble deeper and deeper into our misfortune will depend on whether we accept this spirit or not. This is the "either-or" choice we have. The more people make the decision to turn to this active spirit, the better for the future of humanity.

That is all I wanted to add to today's lecture.

Notes

LECTURE ONE

1. The Goetheanum, a wooden building, was designed by Rudolf Steiner and built from 1913 to 1922 with the help of workers and volunteers from all over Europe. In 1920, the Anthroposophical Society and School of Spiritual Science could begin using the building even though the interior was not yet completely finished. On New Year's Eve 1922, this first Goetheanum was destroyed by fire. Rudolf Steiner created the model for the second Goetheanum, which was built of concrete and completed in 1928/29.

2. The term *cultural-spiritual* corresponds to the German word *Geistesleben*. It includes the areas usually designated by the terms culture, art, humanities, spirituality, and religion.

3. Friedrich Nietzsche, 1844-1900, German philosopher and poet. Professor of classical philology, Basel (1869-79). Opponent of Schopenhauer's philosophy. Known for denouncing religion, for espousing doctrine of perfectibility of man through forcible self-assertion, and for glorification of the superman (*Übermensch*).

4. Nietzsche entitled his essays on the ancient Greek philosophers *Philosophy in the Tragic Age of the Greeks*.

5. Rudolf Steiner, *An Outline of Occult Science*, repr., (Hudson, NY: Anthroposophic Press, 1989) and *Knowledge of the Higher Worlds and Its Attainment*, repr., (Hudson, NY: Anthroposophic Press, 1986).

6. Nicolaus Copernicus, 1473-1543, Polish astronomer. Made astronomical observations of orbits of sun, moon, planets (from

1497); gradually abandoned the universally accepted Ptolemaic system of astronomy and worked out a heliocentric system in which the earth rotates daily on its axis and, with other planets, revolves around the sun.

Galileo Galilei, 1564-1642, Italian mathematician, astronomer, and physicist. First to use telescope to study the skies. Tried by the Inquisition for supporting the Copernican system.

Sir Isaac Newton, 1642-1727, English physicist and mathematician. Conceived the idea of universal gravitation. Discovered the composite nature of white light and the ability of a prism to separate colors owing to their different refrangibilities.

7. Steiner here refers to Friedrich Traub, author of *Rudolf Steiner als Philosoph und Theosoph* ("Rudolf Steiner as Philosopher and Theosophist"), Tübingen 1919.

8. Giordano Bruno, 1548-1600, Italian philosopher. Arrested by the Inquisition and burned at the stake. A critic of Aristotelian logic and champion of Copernican cosmology, which he extended with the notion of the infinite universe.

Wilhelm Conrad Röntgen, 1845-1923, German physicist. Awarded first Nobel prize for physics (1901) for his discovery (1895) of X rays.

Antoine-César Becquerel, 1788-1878, French physicist. One of the creators of the science of electrochemistry.

9. Robert Wilbrandt, German professor. His book *Sozialismus* ("Socialism") (Jena 1919) concludes with the words: "And socialism, if it is ever realized, will cultivate Christianity, which is preached nowadays but is still a foreign element in the world as a need of society" (p. 338).

10. Ottokar Graf von Czernin, 1872-1932, Austro-Hungarian politician. In foreign service (from 1895). As Austro- Hungarian minister to Romania (1913-16) endeavored to prevent Romania from entering World War I. Minister of foreign affairs (1916-18); attempted to extricate Austria- Hungary from World War I; had to resign his office. Author of *Im Weltkrieg* ("In the World War") (1919).

144

11. The name of the lecturer and the topic of the lecture could not be ascertained.

LECTURE TWO

1. Johann Wolfgang von Goethe, 1749-1832, German poet. Also wrote extensively on botany, optics, and other scientific topics.

2. Rudolf Steiner, *Von Seelenrätseln* ("On the Riddles of the Soul"), vol. 21 in the Collected Works, (Dornach, Switzerland: Rudolf Steiner Verlag, 1983). Not translated.

3. See Lecture One, note 5.

LECTURE THREE

1. Arthur Schopenhauer, 1788-1860, German philosopher. Chief expounder of pessimism and of the irrational impulses of life arising from the will. The comment cited reads as follows: "It turns out that preaching morality is easy, but establishing a foundation for it is difficult." It can be found in volume 12 of Schopenhauer's *Complete Works*, Stuttgart and Berlin, 1894.

2. Immanuel Kant, 1724-1804, German philosopher. Developed his own critical philosophy in which he sought to determine the nature and limits of human knowledge, the necessary categories of consciousness, and their ethical and aesthetic consequences. He wrote his *Critique of Pure Reason* in 1781 (rev. 1787) and *Critique of Practical Reason* in 1788. The passage Steiner refers to reads: "Two things fill the mind with ever new and increasing admiration and awe, the oftener and more steadily we reflect on them: the starry heavens above me and the moral law within me." *Critique of Practical Reason*, translated by Lewis White Beck, New York: Liberal Arts Press, 1956, p. 166.

3. See Lecture One, note 5.

4. Johann Wolfgang von Goethe, *Faust* (1808-32), a drama.

5. Kant developed his categorical imperative in his *Critique of*

Practical Reason. It reads as follows: "So act that the maxim of your will could always hold at the same time as a principle establishing universal law." Op. cit., p. 30.

6. Rudolf Steiner, *Philosophy of Freedom: A Philosophy of Spiritual Activity,* vol. 4 in the Collected Works (London: Rudolf Steiner Press, 1988).

7. The passage Steiner refers to reads: "Duty! Thou sublime and mighty name that dost embrace nothing charming or insinuating but requirest submission. . . ." *Critique of Practical Reason,* op. cit., p. 89.

8. Friedrich von Schiller, 1759-1805, German poet, playwright, and critic. Wrote *Letters on the Aesthetic Education of Man* (1795).

9. See Friedrich von Schiller, *Poems,* "The Philosopher: Scruples of Conscience."

10. Johann Wolfgang von Goethe, *Verses in Prose.*

11. See Lecture One, note 6.

12. Rudolf Steiner, *Towards Social Renewal: Basic Issues of the Social Question,* vol. 23 in the Collected Works (London: Rudolf Steiner Press, 1977).

13. See Lecture One, note 8.

14. Erich Wasmann, 1859-1931, Jesuit and entomologist. Studied the life of ants.

15. Steiner here refers to Friedrich Traub, a professor in Tübingen, Germany, who had spoken out against Steiner.

16. Steiner here refers to the Canon Laun who gave a lecture on theosophy and Christianity in Stuttgart in November 1919.

LECTURE FOUR

1. John Maynard Keynes, 1883-1946, English economist. On staff of the Treasury (1915-19) and its principal representative at the Paris Peace conference (1919). Published *The Economic Consequences of the Peace* (1919) arguing against the excessive reparations required of Germany. Played central role in British war finance during World War II. Chief British representative at

Bretton Woods Conference (1944) that established the International Monetary Fund. Known for his revolutionary economic theory that recovery from a recession is best achieved by a government-sponsored policy of full employment.

2. Woodrow Wilson, 1856-1924. Twenty-eighth president of the United States (1913-21). Formulated (Jan. 1918) Fourteen Points plan for peace; plan accepted by Germany (Oct. 1918) and reluctantly by Allies, leading to Armistice (Nov. 11, 1918). Personally participated in Versailles Peace conference and forced acceptance of the League of Nations covenant as an integral part of the treaty of peace. Awarded Nobel peace prize for 1919.

3. Georges Clemenceau, 1841-1929, French politician. Premier of France (1906-09); carried out law separating church and state. Again premier (1917-20), led France through critical days of World War I; headed French delegation to Peace Conference at Paris (1919).

4. David Lloyd George, 1863-1945, British politician. Chancellor of the Exchequer (1908-15); designed (1911) Britain's first comprehensive health and unemployment insurance. Prime minister (1916-22). As virtual dictator directed Britain's policies to victory in World War I and in settlement of terms of peace.

5. See Lecture One, note 5.

6. Johannes Scherr, 1817-1886, German cultural and literary historian. Taught in Zurich, Switzerland.

7. Richard Avenarius, 1843-1896, German philosopher. Professor in Zurich (1877-96); set forth principle of empiriocriticism, a doctrine of undivided pure experience in relation to environment and knowledge.

8. Ernst Mach, 1838-1916, Austrian physicist and philosopher. Investigated the physiology and psychology of the senses, especially in relation to the theory of knowledge. One of the founders of *Empiriokritizismus*, a realistic philosophy based on the analyses of sensations. Established basic principles of modern scientific positivism. Studied flight of projectiles, his name given to ratio of the speed of an object to the local speed of sound.

Friedrich Adler, 1879-1960, student of Mach. Leading Austromarxist and follower of empiriocriticism. Tried to complement Marxism with Mach's philosophy. Assassinated Austrian prime minister Count Karl von Stürgkh; sentenced to death. Sentence was later commuted, and he was released in 1918.

9. Vladimir Ilich Lenin, 1870-1924, Russian Communist leader. Became Marxist (1889), lived in Western Europe (1900-1917); became leader of Bolsheviks. In Russia (from April 1917), assumed leadership of revolutionary movement; overthrew Kerensky's provisional government. Became head of Soviet government and established the dictatorship of the proletariat.

Leon Trotsky, 1879-1940, Russian Communist leader. Exiled to Siberia, fled Russia. Engaged in revolutionary activities while traveling in Europe and U.S. Rejoined Lenin, whom he had met in England (1902) after February Revolution (1917). Became commissar for foreign affairs in Soviet government (1917). After Lenin's death (1924), was defeated in contest with Stalin for control of the Communist party. Expelled from party (1927) and banished from Russia (1929). Lived in Mexico (1937) until murdered.

10. Steiner's assessment is based on an essay by Nicolay A. Berdyayev entitled, "The Political and Philosophical Truth," which was published in German in 1918.

11. In the discussion preceding Steiner's concluding remarks, the first speaker from the audience talked about the efforts to introduce an international language, Esperanto. The second member of the audience to take the floor asked Steiner about the prospect of getting out of the chaos of the times.

12. See Lecture Three, note 12.

13. See Lecture Three, note 6.

LECTURE FIVE

1. See Lecture Two, note 1.

2. See Lecture One, note 5.

3. Emil Molt, 1876-1936, director of the Waldorf-Astoria cigarette factory in Stuttgart, Germany. On his suggestion, the first Waldorf school was founded there as a free school for the children of the employees and others.

4. See Lecture Four, note 9.

5. Ernst Heinrich Haeckel, 1834-1919, German biologist and natural philosopher.

6. Johann Wolfgang von Goethe, "Winckelmann and His Age," in *Essays on Art and Literature*, John Gearey, ed. Translated by Ellen von Nardroff and Ernest H. von Nardroff. New York: Suhrkamp Publishers, 1986, p. 104.

7. Ibid., p. 101.

8. *Dreigliederung des sozialen Organismus* ("Journal for Threefolding of the Social Organism"), founded in July 1919. It was discontinued in June 1922.

9. Pyotr Alekseyevich Kropotkin, 1842-1921, Russian geographer, revolutionist, and philosopher. Made explorations in Siberia, Finland, and Manchuria (1871-73). Joined extreme branch of International Workingmen's Association (1872). Became foremost leader and theorist of anarchist movement. Imprisoned in France. Lived in England (1886-1917) and in Russia (1917-21). Developed theory of "anarchist communism" based on replacement of private property and unequal incomes with free distribution of goods and services. His book *Ethics* was published posthumously in 1922.

RECOVERING
THE SOURCES OF MEANING

Anthroposophy is not just an abstract philosophy but a living spiritual path that reconnects human beings to the universe and to the sources of what it means to be human. Rudolf Steiner, who renewed this path of meaning in our time, saw four of his books as fundamental to the recovery of human dignity. Despite the many other books he wrote, and the more than 6,000 lectures he gave, Steiner returned again and again to these four basic books.

The Philosophy of Spiritual Activity

This fundamental work of philosophy demonstrates the fact of freedom. Read properly, the book leads the reader to experience the living thinking by which all human activity may be renewed.

Knowledge of the Higher Worlds and its Attainment

This fundamental guide to the anthroposophical path of knowledge. Steiner details the exercises and moral qualities to be cultivated on the path to conscious experience of super-sensible realities.

Theosophy

This work begins by describing the threefold nature of the human being. A profound discussion of reincarnation and karma follows, concluding with a description of the soul's journey through the supersensible regions after death.

An Outline of Occult Science

This masterwork places humanity at the heart of the vast, invisible processes of cosmic evolution. Descriptions of the different members of the human being, are followed by a profound investigation of cosmic evolution.

For prices and a catalogue of the more than 300 titles published and distributed by the Anthroposophic Press, please write to:

Anthroposophic Press
RR4, Box 94-A1
Hudson, NY 12534

518-851-2054